Flann O'Brien, Bakhtin, and Menippean Satire

Richard Fallis, *Series Editor*

Flann O'Brien, Bakhtin, and Menippean Satire

M. Keith Booker

Syracuse University Press

The paper used in this publication meets the minimum requirements
of American National Standard for Information Sciences—Permanence
of Paper for Printed Library Materials, ANSI Z39.48-1984. ∞™

Library of Congress Cataloging-in-Publication Data

Booker, M. Keith.
    Flann O'Brien, Bakhtin, and Menippean satire / M. Keith Booker.
        p.   cm. — (Irish studies)
    Includes bibliographical references and index.
    ISBN 0-8156-2665-7
    1. O'Brien, Flann, 1911–1966–Criticism and interpretation.
2. Bakhtin, M. M. (Mikhail Mikhaĭlovich), 1895–1975. 3. Satire,
English—Irish authors—History and criticism. 4. Satire—Classical
influences. 5. Ireland—In literature. I. Title. II. Series:
Irish studies (Syracuse, N.Y.)
PR6029.N56Z55   1995
828'.91209–dc20   95-2468

For Dubravka, Adam, and Milja

M. Keith Booker is an associate professor of English at the University of Arkansas. In addition to his Ph.D. in English, Professor Booker holds degrees in physics and mathematics and in materials science and engineering. He has published over one hundred scientific and technical articles in refereed professional journals such as *Transactions of the American Nuclear Society*. He has also published extensively in literary journals in this country and abroad, and he is the author of several books, including *Techniques of Subversion in Modern Literature: Transgression, Abjection, and the Carnivalesque, Literature and Domination: Sex, Knowledge, and Power in Modern Fiction, Vargas Llosa among the Postmodernists,* and *The Dystopian Impulse in Modern Literature: Fiction as Social Criticism*.

Contents

Acknowledgments

I would like to thank Michael Heffernan and José Lanters for reading
and usefully commenting upon the manuscript of this book. I would
also like to thank Brandon Kershner, who originally made me aware of
Flann O'Brien's work while I was his graduate student at the University
of Florida. Most of all I would like to thank Dubravka Juraga—for
everything.

An earlier version of chapter 1 was originally published as "The Bicycle and Descartes: Epistemology in the Fiction of Beckett and O'Brien"
in *Éire-Ireland* 26.1 (1991): 76–94. Chapter 3 is a revision of "Science,
Philosophy, and *The Third Policeman*: Flann O'Brien and the Epistemology of Futility," published in *South Atlantic Review* 56.4 (1991): 37–56.
An earlier version of chapter 4 was originally published as "O'Brien
Among the Benighted Gaels: Linguistic Oppression and Cultural Definition in Ireland" in *Discours Social/Social Discourse* 3 (Special Bakhtin Number, Spring–Summer 1990): 167–82. Chapter 6 is a revision of *"The
Dalkey Archive*: Flann O'Brien's Critique of Mastery," published in *Irish
University Review*. I would like to thank these journals and their editors
for permission to print the revised versions of these essays in this volume.

Finally, I would like to thank the following: Walker and Company
for permission to quote from *At Swim-Two-Birds* and *The Third Policeman*; A. M. Heath for permission to quote from *The Poor Mouth* and *The
Hard Life* in the United States; HarperCollins Publishers for permission
to quote from *The Poor Mouth* and *The Hard Life* in the British Com-
monwealth; and Dalkey Archive Press for permission to quote from *The
Dalkey Archive*.

Flann O'Brien, Bakhtin, and Menippean Satire

1

O'Brien, Bakhtin, and the
Menippean Tradition

It has by now become a critical commonplace to think of Flann O'Brien along with James Joyce and Samuel Beckett as the three great Irish fiction writers of the twentieth century, though it is certainly also true that O'Brien is almost universally considered the third in this trio. O'Brien is indeed very much an Irish writer, and his work resonates not only with that of contemporaries like Joyce and Beckett but also with the long history of what Vivian Mercier calls the "Irish comic tradition." Many elements of O'Brien's work participate in this tradition, including his sometimes biting satire, his use of the fantastic, his plays with language, and his frequent use of excremental imagery. But these same elements also recall the tradition of Menippean satire, especially as described by Mikhail Bakhtin, and reading O'Brien's fiction within the context of Menippean satire can greatly illuminate many elements of his work.

Many aspects of Bakhtin's work, especially as it relates to Menippean satire, will be elaborated in the course of my readings of O'Brien throughout this book. Bakhtin himself presents a succinct description of Menippean satire in *Problems of Dostoevsky's Poetics,* where he lists fourteen principal characteristics of the genre. O'Brien's work shows all fourteen characteristics, as I summarize in the Appendix. For now, it is sufficient to note that Menippean satire contains by its very nature a diverse collection of competing styles and voices, that it tends to interrogate and satirize various philosophical ideas (usually in a highly irreverent way), and that it is centrally informed by the energies that Bakhtin refers to as "carnivalesque." Bakhtin bases this metaphor on the medieval carnival, a celebration during which normal rules and hierarchies were inverted or

1

suspended and in which representatives of various social groups inter-mixed far more freely than in normal life. The first and most fundamental characteristic of the carnival (and therefore of Menippean satire) is its ambivalence—different points of view, different worlds, may be mutually and simultaneously present without any privileging of one over the other, so that the different worlds can comment on each other in a dia-logic way.

Once an obscure genre, Menippean satire has risen to new critical prominence in the past few decades. Among Anglo-American critics, this resurgence was initiated by Northrop Frye, who identified in the late fifties the Menippean satire (or "anatomy," as he preferred to call it) as one of the principal genres of fiction. Frye's importance is well-known, and one need only cite Philip Stevick's suggestion in 1968 that Frye's genre classification scheme was the "single most significant and influen-tial event in the criticism of prose fiction in the last twenty years" as an indication of the impact that Frye's work had in the years after the pub-lication of his own anatomy (153). But even more important in recent years has been the privileging of Menippean satire by Bakhtin, who did much of his work on the genre in the 1930s in the Soviet Union, but whose work was virtually unknown in the West (or, for that matter, in the Soviet Union itself) until the 1960s, when Bakhtin emerged as a major forerunner of both structuralism and poststructuralism. Bakhtin's theories of language lead directly to later developments in the theory of intertextuality as exemplified by the work of theorists like Julia Kristeva and Jacques Derrida; Paul de Man has suggested that Bakhtin is a justi-fied candidate for the role of "hero" in the modern development of the theory of narrative, particularly as concerns the novel (106–7).[1]

It should be noted that Bakhtin's own account of literary history identifies Menippean satire—as exemplified in the work of Rabelais and others—as the major generic site of carnivalesque energies in literature only until the eighteenth century, when this role shifts to the emerging novel. But Bakhtin's work on Menippean satire is inseparable from his work on the novel because the types of novels privileged by Bakhtin are still centrally informed by Menippean energies. For him the novel is a special genre, unique in its contemporaneity, its contact with everyday life, its close connection with extraliterary genres. Bakhtin's theory is

1. Bakhtin's work has been so widely influential in recent years that a virtual "Bakhtin industry" of criticism and commentary has sprung up around his work. Important general surveys of Bakhtin's work include the critical biography of Clark and Holquist and the studies by Todorov, Morson and Emerson, and Holquist. Also see the collections of essays edited by Morson, Morson and Emerson, and Hirschkop.

founded on language; he argues that the distinguishing feature of the novel as a genre is the way it incorporates the various "languages" of society into its own discourse: "Diversity of voices and heteroglossia enter the novel and organize themselves within it into a structured artistic system. This constitutes the distinguishing feature of the novel as a genre" (*Dialogic* 300). But the languages in a novel have specific sociopolitical connotations as well, each language representing an entire worldview. Bakhtin's key concept of "heteroglossia" refers not just to the words used by different groups in society but to the entire social, cultural, and ideological context of the novel. In the novel, the languages interact in a dynamic way, typically with the development of an opposition between "high" languages and "low." The dialogue in the novel thus dramatizes ideological struggles in the society as a whole.

Bakhtin defines two stylistic lines of development in the novel, the first, which is single-voiced, as in traditional realistic novels, and the second, which is far richer. The Second Line novel, related to Menippean satire, strives for "generic, encyclopedic comprehensiveness," including the heavy use of inserted genres, which "serve the basic purpose of introducing heteroglossia *into* the novel, of introducing an era's many and diverse languages." It embodies the view that "the novel must be a full and comprehensive reflection of its era . . . the novel must represent all the social and ideological voices of its era, that is, all the era's languages that have any claim to being significant; the novel must be a microcosm of heteroglossia" (*Dialogic* 110–11). This dialogic Second Line can easily be traced back to Cervantes and Sterne, but its roots go back even further.

Also important to Bakhtin's conception of the novel is the idea of the carnival. Julia Kristeva (who identifies Bakhtin as an important precursor of her own work on intertextuality) discusses the highly "carnivalesque" character of many novels that derive primarily from this Second Line, which she refers to as "subversive," or "polyphonic" novels, noting their close affinity with Menippean satire. "Carnivalesque," however, does not connote frivolity. "The laughter of the carnival is not simply parodic; it is no more comic than tragic; it is both at once, one might say that it is *serious*" ("Word" 50). She writes that "Menippean discourse develops in times of opposition against Aristotelianism, and writers of polyphonic novels seem to disapprove of the very structures of official thought founded on formal logic." In the subversive novel "identity, substance, causality and definition are transgressed so that others may be adopted: analogy, relation, opposition, and therefore dialogism and Menippean ambivalence" (55–56).

Kristeva's emphasis on subversion indicates the emancipatory tone of much of Bakhtin's rhetoric, which has been criticized by some commentators as taking an overly sanguine view of the political power of parody and polyphony. After all, the medieval carnival on which Bakhtin places so much metaphorical emphasis was itself a sanctioned form of "transgression" whose very purpose was to sublimate and defuse the social tensions that might lead to genuine subversion—a sort of opiate of the masses. Terry Eagleton is only one of many who have pointed out this fact: "Carnival, after all, is a *licensed* affair in every sense, a permissible rupture of hegemony, a contained popular blow-off as disturbing and relatively ineffectual as a revolutionary work of art" (148, Eagleton's emphasis). In addition, while official authority may have typically been the nominal target of most transgressions in the medieval carnival, the actual victims of carnivalesque violence and abuse were quite frequently members of marginal social groups who served as surrogate representatives of official power.[2] One should view Bakhtin's descriptions of the political power of Menippean literary texts with such caveats in mind.

In addition, despite Bakhtin's importance to contemporary literary critics, it should also be noted that his own survey of literary history ends with the work of Dostoevsky, which Bakhtin views as the apotheosis of Menippean energies in the novel. Bakhtin is almost entirely silent on the work of later authors, at least partially because Bakhtin seems to have felt that such energies were on the wane in his own century.[3] But this silence on contemporary literature can largely be explained in terms of official censorship under the Stalinist regime in Soviet Russia, which often made it difficult to discuss contemporary authors, especially Western ones. For example, Bakhtin never mentions Joyce, whose works have frequently been cited as among the best examples of carnivalesque, Menippean texts in the twentieth century.[4] This omission seems striking, but (as Clark and Holquist point out) the official condemnation of Joyce at the 1934 Soviet Writers' Congress meant that "Bakhtin effectively had two choices as regards Joyce, to attack him or not to mention him" (317).

2. On the dark side of the carnival, see Bernstein.
3. For example, Bakhtin sees modern carnivalesque energies as being relatively debased, linking this decline to the Romantic grotesque, noting that here "madness acquires a somber, tragic aspect of individual isolation" (*Rabelais* 39).
4. The Irish tradition associated with writers like Swift, Joyce, and Beckett contains numerous Menippean elements. Joyce has particularly been read as an exemplification of many of Bakhtin's theories of literature and language. Among the many recent Bakhtinian readings of Joyce, see Lodge, White, Valente, and Kershner (*Joyce*). And see my own *Joyce, Bakhtin, and the Literary Tradition*.

Indeed, Clark and Holquist suggest that "virtually all of the great novels of the modern period" centrally participate in the Menippean Second Line of the development of the novel as described by Bakhtin (293). O'Brien's works, with their complex intermixtures of styles and "inserted genres," certainly present excellent examples of the Menippean Second Line novel, placing O'Brien amidst important trends in modern literary history. For example, Max Nänny invokes Bakhtin's work to argue that T. S. Eliot's *Waste Land* can be located within the tradition of Menippean satire or, more generally, within the tradition of carnival (534). Indeed, Nänny sees the trend toward carnivalization, led by Joyce and Eliot, to be one of the major aspects of the entire modernist movement:

> The chief modernist works, Joyce's *Ulysses,* Eliot's *The Waste Land,* and Pound's *Cantos* as well as so much post-modern writing may hence be seen as literary expressions of a pervasive carnivalization of 20th century consciousness and culture, expressions whose strongly ludic character demands an active participation in their carnivalesque games. (534–35)

A great number of the complex, enigmatic products of modern literature have been usefully illuminated through association with the genre of Menippean satire. Such associations are especially important because works of Menippean satire typically appear sloppy and ill-made when viewed within the expectations of other genres. Steven Mailloux notes that when Melville's *Moby-Dick*—itself a Menippean work—was first published in England (as *The Whale*), a reviewer in the *Brittania* wrote that he was "at a loss to determine in what category of works of amusement to place it. It is certainly neither a novel nor a romance, although it is made to drag its weary length through three closely printed volumes, and is published by Bentley, who, *par excellence,* is the publisher of novels of the fashionable world, for who ever heard of a novel or romance without a heroine or a single love scene?" (cited in Mailloux 175). Indeed, much of the reaction to Melville's perplexing book involved puzzled attempts to classify it and thereby render it tame. American reviewers, perhaps less steeped in tradition than their British counterparts, seemed less determined to fit the book into pre-existing categories, but instead were often content to announce it as the beginning of a new genre all its own, calling it such things as an "intellectual chowder," a "Whaliad," and a "prose epic" (Mailloux 176).

O'Brien's work has similarly suffered from a sort of categorical confusion. Typically read within the expectations associated with the conventional novel, O'Brien's work has frequently been found to be somewhat confused, to lack unity, or to lack development of important elements like plot and character.[5] Moreover, following his auspicious debut with the blatantly reflexive *At Swim-Two-Birds,* O'Brien has usually been read as gradually drifting away from experimentalism and toward realism in his later work, even by critics who note with a certain amount of perplexity that his late work doesn't really seem conventionally realistic, either. This narrative of O'Brien's career is usually accompanied by the suggestion that his change in direction was principally triggered by a reaction against the overwhelming influence of Joyce.

The carnivalesque ambivalence of Menippean satire provides an important illumination of the ambivalence of O'Brien's writing, which is consistently comic, even seemingly silly, but which seems informed by a fundamentally dark vision. Indeed, O'Brien's central theme would seem to be the futility of almost all human endeavors in the modern world. But his works also frequently show the kind of exuberant energy normally associated with Menippean satire, suggesting that O'Brien may not be quite as pessimistic as he might seem. Within the dialogic doubleness of Menippean satire, one can read O'Brien's work both as a consistent evocation of the theme of futility and as a parody of such evocations. This doubleness informs all of O'Brien's major works. *At Swim-Two-Birds* is, among other things, an extended demonstration of the ways authors are unable to control the implications of their own writing in the modern world, but the book shows this authorial impotence to have both threatening and liberating implications. *The Third Policeman* can be read as a commentary on the futile efforts of science and philosophy to describe the world through epistemological inquiry—and as a parody of such commentaries. *The Poor Mouth* explores the cultural domination of Ireland that results from the imposition of the English language on the Irish people, but it also explores the complicity of the Irish in their own oppression in ways that suggest possibilities of successful resistance. *The Hard Life* treats the paralysis and sterility of a Dublin culture that seems unable to break out of self-defeating habits of behavior, yet lampoons depictions of the boredom of Dublin life as being every bit as boring as the life they criticize. And *The Dalkey Archive* is an extended deconstruction of various figures and discourses of authority—including itself.

In this book I read these major works within the context of Menip-

5. Ann Clissmann's important book on O'Brien is typical of this tendency to see a lack of unity and structure in O'Brien's later work. Interestingly, she suggests that *At Swim-Two-Birds* "may be a work which would fit Northrop Frye's definition of 'Anatomy'" (89), but she never makes this connection for O'Brien's other works—which she consistently criticizes for their lack of coherence.

pean satire and of Bakhtin's work in general. I begin by placing O'Brien in an Irish context, relating his work particularly to that of Beckett and to the focus of both Beckett and O'Brien on the futility of human epistemological inquiry. However, I then present readings of O'Brien's five major works within the tradition of Menippean satire to demonstrate that O'Brien's vision is not unequivocally pessimistic. I end with a discussion of O'Brien's work within an international context, comparing his work to that of modern writers like Kafka, Conrad, Queneau, García Márquez, and Bulgakov. This study shows that, far from being confused and lacking coherence, O'Brien's texts are informed by the complex, polyphonic energies to be expected of Menippean satire. Moreover, these readings show that—contrary to the usual critical perception—O'Brien maintains a consistently experimental writing practice throughout his career. In particular, all of O'Brien's work is centrally concerned with explorations of the uses and social implications of language. O'Brien's comedy is not silly or gratuitous, but participates in important ways in his ongoing engagement with important social, political, and cultural issues in his contemporary Ireland. Reading O'Brien through Bakhtin's theories of literature and language brings into focus O'Brien's central participation in a number of important trends in modern history—literary and otherwise.

2

Menippean Satire in Ireland
O'Brien, Beckett, and the Futility of Epistemological Inquiry

There is a fascinating scene at the end of Beckett's *Murphy* in which the old, crippled Mr. Kelly (a forerunner of later, more paradigmatic crippled Beckett "heroes" like Malone) flies his kite in the park. Mr. Kelly is a skillful flier, even from his wheelchair, and the kite reaches such heights that it disappears from view, giving its owner an opportunity to engage in some profound epistemological speculations: "Now he could measure the distance from the unseen to the seen, now he was in a position to determine the point at which seen and unseen met" (*Murphy* 280). This is a supreme Beckettian moment, both in its acknowledgment that there is an "unseen" to which human scientific and philosophical investigations simply do not have access and in the futility of Mr. Kelly's attempt to gain a knowledge even of the boundary of the unseen.[1] He falls asleep, the winch slips from his hand, and the kite is lost forever, the crippled Mr. Kelly tottering impotently behind the receding string.

The little epistemological parable with which Beckett ends his first published novel (unless *More Pricks Than Kicks* is a novel) is certainly not unique. Angela Moorjani, for example, has noted the way Mr. Kelly's games with the kite parallel the famous *fort/da* game played by Freud's grandson (83). The episode also bears some interesting similarities to the story of the disappearing balloonist related by the periphrastic Sergeant

1. Though *Murphy* carries on an extensive dialogue with philosophy, Kelly's experiment is placed in a specifically scientific framework through comparison with Adams's deduction of the existence of the unseen Neptune from his observations of the seen Uranus.

Pluck to the nameless narrator of O'Brien's *Third Policeman*. According to Pluck, this balloonist once ascended out of the sight even of telescopes but was missing from the basket when the balloon was pulled back in. So, they sent the balloon back up, and "the second time lo and behold the man was sitting in the basket without a feather out of him" (158). The townspeople are necessarily curious to learn what transpired in the interim, but the man refuses to talk. And when they go after him with guns to force an explanation, he escapes again in the balloon and this time disappears once and for all, like Kelly's kite. Again, O'Brien's epistemological moral seems clear—and similar to that of Beckett. Some things are simply beyond the limits of human knowledge.

Perhaps the parallel here between Beckett and O'Brien is not entirely surprising. Both, after all, are prominent Irish writers (the Beckett of *Murphy* being more identifiably Irish than the Beckett of the later French texts), and Hugh Kenner has pointed out the fascination of Irish writers with epistemology. The great Irish writers, Kenner suggests, "have always been able to regard the human dilemma as essentially an epistemological, not an ethical, comedy" (*Samuel Beckett* 37). There are, in fact, a number of interesting similarities between the work of O'Brien and that of Beckett, especially the earlier Beckett. The two were roughly contemporaries, Beckett being five years older. Both came of age in a post-*Ulysses* Ireland, and both were influenced by the work of Joyce in profound ways. Thus despite certain obvious differences in their backgrounds (Beckett being a Protestant who followed Joyce into exile, O'Brien being a Catholic who stayed in Ireland), one might expect important intertextual relations to exist between the two writers. Yet, relatively little work has been done to explore these relations. Anne Clissmann, in her copious and highly useful study of the work of O'Brien, notes that O'Brien's "vision has much in common with Beckett" (37). But she does not proceed to discuss this commonality in vision, and her approach is typical. Beckett is similarly mentioned in passing at several points in O'Brien criticism, while mentions of O'Brien in Beckett criticism are virtually nonexistent.[2]

There is, however, much to be gained by a more extensive examination of the various similarities (and differences) between O'Brien and Beckett. For one thing, because Beckett is the more prominent of the two, such a study would help to locate O'Brien's place in twentieth-

2. Brian Cosgrove complains that Clissmann particularly fails to mention what he sees as strong parallels between *Watt* and *The Third Policeman*. He then concludes that "it is a major shortcoming of the whole critical venture that O'Brien and his contemporary Beckett are never placed in any meaningful juxtaposition" (123).

century literary history, a place that thus far has not been well defined. For another, because O'Brien is the more obviously Irish of the two, such a study would help to illuminate Beckett's position as an Irish writer and to explicate his dialogue with Irish culture and literature. And both of these advantages are greatly enhanced by the simple fact that numerous parallels between the two authors do exist, so that a comparative study has rich and fertile territory to explore.

O'Brien, in *At Swim-Two-Birds,* depicts a literary world in which characters can freely float from one text to another. Beckett characters constantly migrate from one text to another as well, and certainly one has little trouble envisioning Beckett characters at least up to Watt, and probably up to Malone and Mercier and Camier, sharing the same fictional space with O'Brien characters like Dermot Trellis, Mick Shaughnessy, and the narrators of *At Swim* and *The Third Policeman.* Moreover, there are some striking similarities between the imagery employed by the early Beckett and that used by O'Brien. The fictional worlds of both writers are liberally populated with bicycles, pigs, big dumb Irish policemen, cripples, slothful narrators who lie in bed while constructing their fictions, and abject instances of violence and degradation. Many of these similarities can be attributed to the fact that Beckett's early fiction (and all of O'Brien's) takes place in an identifiably Irish landscape.[3] As a result, one might expect a certain parallelism in the kinds of objects and images that appear in the works of the two writers. This point is not a trivial one, serving as it does to emphasize the importance of Beckett's Irish cultural background. But many of these common images also serve to reinforce the assaults carried out by both writers on the pretensions of epistemology. Both Beckett and O'Brien share an extreme skepticism of human epistemological investigation. To both of them, there is no hope of gaining a direct knowledge and understanding of reality, even in the kinds of special moments of insight referred to by Joyce as epiphanies or by Virginia Woolf as moments of being. Indeed, much that Beckett and O'Brien have in common as writers can be formulated in terms of the efforts of both to debunk the pretensions to a privileged access to reality claimed to inhere in certain special modes of inquiry, including art, philosophy, and sexuality.

Some of the very similarities between O'Brien and Beckett complicate a comparison of their work. Both authors write in more than one language—Beckett in French and English, O'Brien in English and Gae-

---

3. For an interesting discussion of the Irish setting of Beckett's fictions, see Mercier (*Beckett/Beckett* 20–45).

lic. In addition, both authors work in a number of genres and for a variety of media, supplementing fiction with drama and extending drama to include works for television, radio, and film. And finally, both show a considerable amount of artistic evolution in the courses of their careers, with late works bearing little resemblance, at least stylistically, to early ones. In particular, the two writers seem to evolve in different directions, with Beckett continually striving boldly to go where no writer (including himself) has gone before and O'Brien ostensibly retreating into increasingly conventional modes of writing as their two careers developed.[4]

These differences in artistic development between Beckett and O'Brien can be explained in part by their respective reactions to the influence of Joyce on their early careers. Joyce's writing has been prominently identified as paradigmatic of Bakhtin's theories of language and the novel and as a central instance of Menippean satire in modern fiction, and so the link to Joyce helps to place both O'Brien and Beckett in the Menippean tradition. Any comparison of the work of Beckett and O'Brien must begin with a recognition of the extensive impact of the work of Joyce on both writers—many similarities between the two may in fact derive from having Joyce as a common source of inspiration (and exasperation). If early Beckett characters like the slothful Belacqua and the seedy solipsist Murphy bear certain resemblances to such figures from O'Brien as Dermot Trellis and the *At Swim* narrator, both bedridden artists manqué, at least some of that similarity surely arises from the fact that all claim Stephen Dedalus as a literary progenitor.[5] And if the difficulties suffered by Trellis and the *Third Policeman* narrator recall those of all Beckett narrators from Molloy onward, they also echo the tribulations of Leopold Bloom in "Circe" and of HCE in *Finnegans Wake*.

The relationships of both Beckett and O'Brien to Joyce have been extensively discussed, and I have no intention of rehearsing those discussions here, though there is still extensive room for the exploration of those relationships.[6] In particular, our understanding of the work of

4. Ian Mackenzie suggests that O'Brien "seems to be the only writer to have begun his career as a modernist and then reverted to a kind of naturalism" (55).

5. Proust is an obvious predecessor here as well, especially for Beckett, who began his career with an insightful critical book on Proust.

6. The most extensive study of the relationship between Joyce and Beckett is the book-length study by Gluck, though Gluck's understanding of both Joyce and Beckett could use more critical engagement. Other representative studies include those by Cohn, Hayman ("A Meeting" and "Joyce"), and Moses. In addition to Mackenzie, representative studies of Joyce and O'Brien include discussions in Clissmann and articles like those by Browne, Janik, and Mays ("Brian O'Nolan").

Joyce himself has changed dramatically in the last decade or so as we have come increasingly to realize the extent of Joyce's interest in politics and the profound engagement of his writing in his own social and historical moment.[7] For my purposes here, it is sufficient to note that both Beckett and O'Brien were admirers of Joyce early in their careers and that their early styles—marked by a punning, allusive, linguistic exuberance—appear to reflect this admiration.

Both Beckett and O'Brien appear to have regarded Joyce as a figure of artistic mastery, and the later stylistic movements of both writers away from identifiably Joycean writing practices illustrate the disavowal of mastery that informs their later work. If both Beckett and O'Brien are critical of the pretensions of Western epistemology, they are correspondingly skeptical of the typical modernist notion (espoused by a number of commentators on modernism, if not necessarily by the "modernists" themselves) that art, particularly literature, functions as a privileged mode of access to the Truth. Heidegger's definition of art as "the becoming and happening of truth" and his accompanying statement that "the linguistic work, poetry in the narrower sense, has a privileged position in the domain of the arts" are paradigmatic of this belief (183, 185). But Joyce's Stephen Dedalus, with his aesthetics of the epiphany, provides what is perhaps the central modernist statement of art as a privileged mode of epistemology, and it is Stephen's famous depiction in *A Portrait of the Artist as a Young Man* of the artist as an invisible God-like figure distantly paring His fingernails while He overlooks His creation that serves as the paradigm of the artist-as-master, a role that both Beckett and O'Brien decline to play.

To Beckett and O'Brien, the artist is not the grand, God-like figure so often associated with the aesthetics of Stephen and (erroneously, I think) of Joyce himself. Beckett insists in perhaps his central nonfiction portrait of the artist that "to be an artist is to fail, as no other dare fail" (*Disjecta* 145). And O'Brien, in an essay devoted primarily to a discussion of Joyce, likens the typical Irish artist to a drunk who is unknowingly lost in the darkness of a railway tunnel for days, waiting for the coming of dawn ("Bash" 206). There is, however, a clear irony in these protestations of artistic impotence. As Yeats demonstrates in "The Circus Animals' Desertion," it is a common strategy of the Irish artist to create art based on the *topos* of the inability to create art.

Even Joyce's depictions of the pretentious Stephen Dedalus show an

---

7. Important works that have participated in this re-reading of Joyce include those by Manganiello, Herr, and Kershner. Also see my *Joyce, Bakhtin, and the Literary Tradition*.

artist who is unable to create anything significant, and Stephen himself echoes fellow Irish aesthete Oscar Wilde when he suggests that the appropriate "symbol of Irish art" is the "cracked lookingglass of a servant" (*Ulysses* 6). In point of fact, Joyce's work is informed by very much the same skepticism as Beckett's and O'Brien's.[8] But Stephen's demystification of the Irish artist here has a strongly political dimension, referring to the frustrations of the historical domination of Ireland by England. Similarly, the aesthetics of failure in Beckett and O'Brien goes beyond mere artistic mask or fashionable twentieth-century pessimism and speaks directly to political realities in Ireland, a country whose history is fundamentally informed by futility.

O'Brien seems to have been ahead of his time as a Joyce critic in realizing the potential ridiculousness of Stephen's artistic poses, but he seems to have failed to take the additional step of acknowledging the ironic gap between Joyce and his character, never understanding that Joyce himself might have been ridiculing Stephen. O'Brien's critique of Joyce seems motivated by a fundamental equation of Joyce with Stephen, and indeed that critique very often takes the form of direct parodies of Stephen.[9] O'Brien characters like Dermot Trellis, the unnamed narrator in *At Swim-Two-Birds,* and Mick Shaughnessy in *The Dalkey Archive* bear striking resemblances to Joyce's Stephen—much to Stephen's disadvantage. Similarly, O'Brien's depiction of paralytic suffering in works like *The Poor Mouth* and *The Hard Life* comment not only on conditions in Ireland but on Joyce's commentary on those conditions, particularly in *Dubliners.*

Indeed, it seems clear that *Dubliners* and *Portrait* are the Joycean works that are most directly reflected in the work of O'Brien. Obvious allusions to *Ulysses* are rare, except for "Joyce's" denial in *The Dalkey Archive* that he wrote the book. And O'Brien's dislike of *Finnegans Wake* (which he was given to referring to as "Flannagan's Awake") seems to have been so intense that Mackenzie has suggested that it was the excess of Wakean language that drove O'Brien back toward more conventional modes of writing after *At Swim-Two-Birds* (55).

Beckett, much more of an insider in the Joyce circle, seems to have understood Joyce's work, especially the later work, better than did O'Brien. Indeed, one explanation for the different stylistic development

8. In particular, there are numerous similarities between Beckett's aesthetics of failure and Joyce's aesthetics.

9. O'Brien refers to "Stephen Dedalus" as Joyce's "other name" ("Bash" 201). In one of his "Cruiskeen Lawn" columns in the *Irish Times* (June 6, 1957), O'Brien calls *Portrait* "Joyce's extended portrait of himself."

of Beckett and O'Brien might be that the former was most influenced by *Ulysses* and *Finnegans Wake,* as opposed to the latter's emphasis on the earlier Joycean works. Beckett, a featured member of Joyce's handpicked *Our Exagmination* panel, was a leading early apologist for Joyce's last and strangest work, and early Beckett pieces like the story "Assumption" and the unfinished novel *A Dream of Fair to Middling Women* (but also the published books at least through *Watt*) show marked Wakean stylistic influences.

Beckett's ostensibly un-Joycean turn to the spare, hard, crystalline style of his later work functions not so much as a critique of Joyce's failure as an acknowledgment of Joyce's success. Always centrally concerned with the limitations of language, Beckett seems to have realized that the technique of giving language its head, of revelling in the unruliness and abundance of language, had already been pushed by Joyce to its limits. Like his Unnamable, Beckett finds himself unable to go on in the Joycean vein, but he goes on anyway, in a different direction. Indeed, after *The Unnamable,* the relevance of Joyce for reading Beckett becomes more and more oblique. In contrast, O'Brien's resentment toward Joyce never abated, and the figure of Joyce haunts O'Brien's work to the very end of his career. It is telling that O'Brien's last book features Joyce as a character, one who is reduced to mending the underwear of Jesuits as his principal opportunity for creative activity.[10]

O'Brien's undoing of the myth of Joyce as master is paralleled in the texts of Beckett by the tendency of the latter's artist/narrators to undo themselves. Beckett's palinodic texts constantly cancel and contradict themselves, thoroughly undermining any attempt to read them as an expression of insight into the truth. Part 2 of *Molloy* is paradigmatic of this strategy. The section is presented as the "report" of Jacques Moran, a sort of failed private detective, a professional cousin of Camier. As such, the section might be expected to have a certain authoritative truthfulness. It begins: "It is midnight. The rain is beating on the windows" (*Three* 92). Then, with typical Beckettian circularity, the section ends on the same note, with the beginning of the writing of the report itself: "Then I went back to the house and wrote, It is midnight. The rain is beating on the windows." But then the last sentences of the book undercut all that

10. Joyce's desire to be a Jesuit in *The Dalkey Archive* illustrates O'Brien's contention that Joyce must have been a believing Catholic else he would not have felt so compelled to blaspheme against the church. O'Brien's analysis of Joyce clearly echoes Cranly's diagnosis of Stephen in *Portrait.* One might counter, of course, that O'Brien's continuing need to critique Joyce shows a similar ongoing faith in Joyce's greatness. As O'Brien himself puts it, "all true blasphemers must be believers" ("Bash" 202).

has come before: "It was not midnight. It was not raining" (176).[11] Similarly, in the much later *How It Is,* the entire text is presented as a quotation, which should lend it some authority, but then the end denies all that has come before.

The circular text (perhaps showing another Joycean influence) is also a favorite form of O'Brien's. In *The Third Policeman,* the last two pages are largely repetitions of passages that appeared in the book one hundred fifty pages earlier, and the indication is that the action of most of the book will be repeated endlessly. Moreover, this action, consisting largely of the narrator's attempts to avoid execution, is undercut by the revelation two pages from the end that he has been dead all along and that most of the book takes place in a surreal afterworld.[12] That so much of the text at the end of *The Third Policeman* is repeated verbatim from earlier in the book serves to signal not only the futility of the narrator's efforts to break out of his confined condition but also to indicate the inability of the writer to produce anything genuinely new. Numerous passages are repeated in *At Swim-Two-Birds* as well, and a great deal of *The Dalkey Archive* is transcribed verbatim from *The Third Policeman.* One might recall here O'Brien's claim in an *Irish Times* article of June 4, 1945, that he himself "has nothing original to say," and compare Beckett's suggestion that for the artist "there is nothing to express, nothing with which to express, nothing from which to express, no power to express, no desire to express, together with the obligation to express" (*Disjecta* 139).

The infinite repeatability of *The Third Policeman* also brings to mind the nested narratives of *At Swim-Two-Birds. At Swim* is a novel about a writer who is writing a novel, a motif that leads to interesting possibilities. The notebook of Philip Quarles in Aldous Huxley's *Point Counter Point* notes that the topos of a writer writing can be extended indefinitely:

> But why draw the line at one novelist inside your novel? Why not a second inside his? And a third inside the novel of the second? And so on to infinity, like those advertisements of Quaker Oats where there's a

11. Thiher notes the function of *Molloy* as a demonstration of the failure of art: "As a kind of meta-text to the major texts that make up Western culture, *Molloy* demonstrates the inadequacy of all these texts to account for Molloy's misadventures and his pointless narration" (107).

12. Many Beckett characters suspect that they may in fact already be dead. Malone strikingly echoes *The Third Policeman* when he notes that life sometimes seems so strange that you begin "to wonder if you have not died without knowing and gone to hell or been born again into an even worse place than before" (*Three* 227).

> Quaker holding a box of oats, on which is a picture of another Quaker
> holding another box of oats, and on which etc., etc. (302)

More than one critic has pointed out the relevance of Huxley's image of
infinite regression, generally referred to in critical discourse as the *mise en
abyme*, to the work of O'Brien, especially in the nested narratives of *At
Swim-Two-Birds*.[13] And this relevance is no accident; the author/narrator
of the book informs us that he has on his shelves "works ranging from
those of Mr. Joyce to the widely-read books of Mr. A. Huxley, the emi-
nent English writer" (*At Swim* 12).

The conflation of Joyce with Huxley here reminds us that Joyce's
Portrait is a prime illustration of a novel about a writer. Maurice Beebe
reminds us in a well-known essay that the "artist-novel" is a major element of modern fiction, citing Huxley, Joyce, and Proust as exemplars of
the technique (*Ivory Towers*). And if Huxley and Joyce centrally inform
the work of O'Brien, then Proust and Joyce do the same for Beckett, and
so it comes as no surprise that Beckett participates in this trend as well.
Beckett's novels include any number of *mise en abyme* effects, the most
obvious of which are his nested narrations, which, especially in the trilogy, bear some striking resemblances to *At Swim-Two-Birds*. Malone is
apparently the author of earlier Beckett characters like Molloy and Moran
from *Molloy* (as well as his own "characters" in *Malone Dies*), and the
Unnamable is perhaps the author of all Beckett characters before him.

Such nested narrations suggest a potentially infinite regression, creating a vertiginous effect that is even more pronounced when the levels of
the nesting become confused. Thus, the most disorienting effect of *At
Swim-Two-Birds* occurs not because the narrator creates the writer Dermot Trellis who in turn creates the writer Orlick Trellis, but because the
sequence turns on itself when Dermot Trellis's characters disgruntled
Shanahan and Lamont suggest that Orlick Trellis write about his father:

> On investigation, they find that Orlick has inherited his father's gift for
> literary composition. Greatly excited, they suggest that he utilize his gift
> to turn the tables (as it were) and compose a story on the subject of
> Trellis, a fitting punishment indeed for the usage he has given others.
> (*At Swim* 236)

This fundamental transgression serves as an important image of a
lack of artistic mastery. It also sends the potentially infinite regression of
narratives rippling in both directions, making it impossible to determine

13. See Browne (152) and Clissmann (95).

who has created whom. Precisely the same effect occurs in *The Unnamable*. Unlike Malone, who feels confident that Macmann, Moll, Lemuel, and the others about whom he spins narratives, the Unnamable is not sure whether he has created characters like Worm and Mahood, or whether they have in fact created him, or even *are* him, or a variety of other Beckett characters as well. His description of his "physical" location also indicates his ontological predicament: "I like to think I occupy the centre, but nothing is less certain" (*Three* 295).

This uncertain, but infinite, nesting leads to a radical epistemological uncertainty in which it is clearly impossible to determine when any scientific or philosophical investigation into the Truth has in fact "struck bottom." The similarity between O'Brien and Beckett in terms of their mutual fascination with images of infinite regression may again show the commonality of their Irish cultural backgrounds. Noting the self-reflexive implication of the title trope in Joyce's *Portrait*, Kenner remarks that the self-portrait motif "holds the mirror up to a mirror" and compares this reflexive situation with Swift's *Tale of a Tub*, Beckett's *Malone Dies,* and Yeats's "Phases of the Moon":

> This theme, "mirror on mirror mirroring all the show," has been since at least Swift's time an inescapable mode of the Irish literary imagination, which is happiest when it can subsume ethical notions into an epistemological comedy. ("Cubist" 172)[14]

This motif also again speaks to the dialogue of both Beckett and O'Brien with Descartes. The fundamental Cartesian cogito involves the situation of a mind thinking of itself thinking—precisely the sort of self-referential situation that, like Huxley's Quaker Oats box, leads to infinite regression. Yet on the assumption that his own process of thought is itself beyond doubt, Descartes takes that as a starting point and then regenerates everything else from there, including (in an odd reversal of creator and created) God. This ability of Descartes to find an origin of all knowledge in the human mind is crucial to the sort of epistemological philosophy that has come to be associated with his name. But the self-referentiality of the Cartesian cogito is clear: perhaps Descartes only *thinks* he thinks, and so on. And if God exists because Descartes thinks He exists, then perhaps Descartes only exists because some meta-Descartes thinks him. The *mise en abyme* motif thus provides the perfect cri-

14. Kenner's mirror metaphor recalls the experiment performed by de Selby in *The Third Policeman*, which involves an arrangement wherein one mirror is reflected within another, leading to an infinite regression of images (*Third* 65).

tique of Cartesian epistemology by demonstrating that all knowledge does not in fact emanate from a locatable origin, but is simply produced as a by-product of an endlessly ongoing inquiry.

Descartes is an important figure in the dialogues of both Beckett and O'Brien with epistemological inquiry. For if Joyce stands as emblematic of the supposed ability of art to reach the Truth, then Descartes plays the same role for philosophy. Cartesian dualism functions as an important structural device in almost all of Beckett's fiction, and it informs the work of O'Brien as well. For example, the encounter between the Pooka McPhellimey and the Good Fairy in *At Swim-Two-Birds* is very much an encounter, however parodic, between the flesh and the spirit, analogous to a similar dialogue set up in Beckett's story "Dante and the Lobster." Similarly, in *The Third Policeman* the narrator conducts an ongoing dialogue (somewhat along the lines of Yeats's "Dialogue of the Self and Soul") with his soul, named "Joe."[15] This fundamental split in the narrator's self is reminiscent of the more profound self-estrangement suffered by almost all Beckett characters, like the narrator of "The Expelled," "whose soul writhed from morning to night, in the mere quest of itself" (*Stories* 11).

But Beckett's characters, despite the inner direction of most of their quests, do not really bear out the neat Cartesian distinction between self and not-self because they are ultimately as alienated from their inner minds as from their outer bodies. Beckett's self-conscious narrators constantly *think*, but they are not at all sure that they therefore *are*. For example, the narrator of *Texts for Nothing 1* sets up a duality between the head and the body, then denies them both: "I should turn away from it all, away from the body, away from the head, let them work it out between them" (*Stories* 75). Similarly, the narrator of *The Third Policeman* has a mind independent of Joe, and there is a hint that Joe might even have a body independent of the narrator, leading to another infinite regression that topples the Cartesian hope of finding a foundation for epistemological inquiry in the stability of the human self:

> What if he *had* a body? A body with another body inside it in turn, thousands of such bodies within each other like the skins of an onion, receding to some unimaginable ultimum? Was I in turn merely a link in

15. The resonance between Yeats and O'Brien is quite rich here. In Yeats's poem, the "self" rejects the turning away from physical life offered by the "soul" and declares a willingness to "live it all again." O'Brien's narrator will also continually relive the events of the book, the difference being that he is repeating death, not life, showing the typical O'Brien hesitance to affirm life.

a vast sequence of imponderable beings, the world I knew merely the interior of the being whose inner voice I myself was? Who or what was the core and what monster in what world was the final uncontained colossus? God? Nothing? (*Third* 118)

Similarly, Beckett characters are frequently faithful Cartesians, but their dogged attempts to follow Cartesianism through to its logical end invariably meet with dire consequences. For example, Malone undergoes a Cartesian program of radical doubt, but unlike Descartes, he is unable to find a stable ground in the fixity of the epistemological self. Malone thinks a great deal but finds therein no guarantee of his absolute existence:

But what matter whether I was born or not, have lived or not, am dead or merely dying, I shall go on doing as I have always done, not knowing what it is I do, nor who I am, nor where I am, nor if I am. (*Three* 226)

There is no room here to discuss the full dialogue with Descartes of either O'Brien or (especially) Beckett, but a single example will suffice to illustrate some of the commonality in both philosophical interests and artistic imagery of the two writers. The unusual prominence of bicycles in O'Brien and Beckett can partially be explained by the simple fact that bicycles were an extremely common mode of transportation in early twentieth-century Ireland—Dublin, as Mackenzie so charmingly puts it, "used to be one of the most bicycle-ridden towns in the world" (63). Yet, bicycles in both Beckett and O'Brien seem to fill consistent symbolic roles that go beyond mere realism. As Kenner has noted, bicycles in Beckett tend to function as representations of the physical side of the Cartesian duality, their smooth mechanical efficiency standing in for the clocklike body envisioned by Descartes and in contrast to the inefficient, decaying body of human reality and of Beckett's fiction (*Samuel Beckett* 117–32). Indeed, Beckett's characters often seem to use bicycles as explicit substitutes for physicality, whether it be in Moran's commissioning of a bicycle to take the place of his failing legs or in Belacqua's preference of a stolen bicycle to stolen kisses from his girlfriend Winnie.

Perhaps Beckett's most dramatic contrast between the mechanical perfection of the bicycle and the sad imperfection of the human body comes in the slapstick-but-somehow-vaguely-heroic efforts of Molloy to balance his grotesque form atop his unusual chainless bicycle:

> I fastened my crutches to the cross-bar, one on either side, I propped the foot of my stiff leg (I forget which, now they're both stiff) on the projecting front axle, and I pedalled with the other. (*Three* 16)

This is quintessential Beckett, yet it is also a scene that would not be at all out of place in the work of O'Brien, especially in *The Third Policeman*.

Mackenzie suggests that bicycles play symbolic roles in O'Brien similar to those in Beckett (63). However, if the rider/bicycle relationship in O'Brien serves as an image of Cartesian dualism, it is a highly carnivalesque one that deconstructs the normal mind/body hierarchy—rider and bicycle are, in O'Brien, not so easy to distinguish. This deconstruction of Cartesian dualities is most memorably figured in *The Third Policeman* in Sergeant Pluck's "Atomic Theory," which argues that the atoms of bicycles and their riders tend to intermingle, to the point that the riders themselves may become more bicycle than human, while the bicycles become more human than machine. O'Brien himself was so pleased with this motif that he repeated it almost verbatim more than two decades later in the "Mollycule Theory" of Sergeant Fottrell in *The Dalkey Archive* (87–97).[16] My reading of this theory as a deconstruction of Cartesian dualism is then strengthened by the fact that Descartes is the direct object of a considerable amount of satire in the later book.[17]

In addition to their propensity to become human, bicycles in O'Brien are also far from perfect as machines. A bicycle's weak point, of course, is its tires, and O'Brien's bicycles tend to have flats almost constantly. In *The Dalkey Archive*, Sergeant Fottrell spends most of his time purposely puncturing the tires of his constituents to minimize their riding and thus to prevent them from becoming bicycles. The narrator of *The Third Policeman* has trouble keeping his tires inflated as well, and Mr. Mathers is felled by a blow from an iron bicycle-pump, which thus functions as a sort of reminder of mortality (*Third* 16).[18] But bicycles are far from perfect in Beckett as well. When Molloy relocates his bicycle preparatory to an attempted escape from *chez Lousse*, he discovers that it will not serve: "But I pushed and pulled in vain, the wheels would not

16. Though completed by early 1940, *The Third Policeman* was not published until after O'Brien's death. Thinking it would *never* be published, O'Brien reused much of the material from *The Third Policeman* when he wrote *The Dalkey Archive* in the 1960s, providing (perhaps inadvertently) an illustration of the model of the novel as being constructed from pre-existing material put forth by the narrator of *At Swim-Two-Birds* (33).

17. Both De Selby (16) and St. Augustine (42) revile Descartes in *The Dalkey Archive*.

18. Compare the rusty bicycle pump that lies in the garden of Joyce's "Araby," functioning as an image of the fall from an Edenic past (*Dubliners* 29).

turn. It was as though the brakes were jammed, and heaven knows they were not, for my bicycle had no brakes" (*Three* 47).

Similarly, the second-hand bicycle obtained by Moran's son has seen better days: "it must once have been quite a good bicycle" (*Three* 155). That bicycles, too, are prey to the decay of the flesh in Beckett is especially emphasized in *Mercier and Camier*, where the title players are relatively healthy as Beckett characters go—but their bicycle becomes sadly crippled and decayed:

> Of it there remains, said Mercier, securely chained to the railing, as much as may reasonably remain, after a week's incessant rain, of a bicycle relieved of both wheels, the saddle, the bell and the carrier. And the tail-light, he added, I nearly forgot. (*Mercier* 85)

Both Beckett and O'Brien use bicycles as important symbols for entering into subversive dialogues with Cartesian dualism. Indeed, these parallel bicycle passages point toward the way both Beckett and O'Brien employ a number of philosophical systems as important elements of their fiction, generally in such a way as to undermine those systems.

Philosophy has long been recognized as an important entry-point into the fiction of Beckett, and a number of philosophical explications of his work can be found in the literature—based on the thinking of a wide range of figures, including Descartes, Geulincx, Berkeley, Leibnitz, Vico, Schopenhauer, Wittgenstein, and Mauthner. Beckett's work invites such readings in certain obvious ways, including the foregrounding of philosophical thought that occurs in *Murphy* and the virtual catalogue of philosophical approaches that can be found in *The Unnamable*.[19] Yet, Beckett himself showed a certain irritation with the prevalence of such readings, once claiming in an interview that he never read philosophers because "I never understand anything they write."

Such protestations must be taken with a grain of salt, of course, but Beckett's comment does point to the way his work engages, rather than illustrates the philosophical systems it has been shown to involve. Thus, Sylvie Debevec Henning reads Beckett's work within the demystifying tradition of Menippean satire, noting for example that *Murphy*, Beckett's parodic novel of ideas, "does not so much embody a specific philosophy as satirize what is perhaps the dominant strain of the Western tradition: a general faith in the reality, or possibility, of ultimate identity or totality"

19. Fletcher notes that The Unnamable "raises most of the disputed issues of technical philosophy and poses them in dramatic terms" (191).

(29). Mercier sees a similar skepticism toward the pretensions of philosophy in *Watt:*

> The philosophers' quest for "truth"—a word most contemporary philosophers would not dare to use—or for something theoretically easier to find, such as an agreed terminology, is the comic image that underlies many pages of *Watt* and gives the book whatever unity it possesses. (*Beckett/Beckett* 169)[20]

These suggestions point toward the principal affinity between Beckett and O'Brien in their use of philosophy, that being a mutual suspicion of the philosophical drive toward mastery, and particularly a deep-seated skepticism concerning the ability of epistemological inquiry to reach a definitive answer in relation to any of the questions it pursues. Indeed, both treat philosophy very much in the tradition of Menippean satire. Granted, such antiphilosophical skepticism is itself a common philosophical notion, as thinkers from Nietzsche to Derrida have prominently shown. For Beckett, perhaps the most important philosophical antecedent to this mode of thought was the Austrian empiricist Fritz Mauthner. Linda Ben-Zvi notes that Mauthner preceded Beckett in acknowledging the certainty of epistemological failure in his own philosophical enterprise:

> Such certain failure did not deter Mauthner, as it did not deter Beckett: both place "the fidelity to failure" at the center of their works and see their major task as promoting recognition of the basic condition of human experience—"unknown and unknowable." (187)

The radical epistemological skepticism of Beckett is well known. It is perhaps figured most clearly in the failed quests of travelers like Molloy and Moran and Mercier and Camier and in the general alienation of his characters from language and from themselves, is well known. Molloy expresses the typical Beckettian dilemma of belated perception and mediated expression of knowledge through language:

> And even my sense of identity was wrapped in a namelessness often hard to penetrate . . . . And so on for all the other things which made merry with my senses. Yes, even then, when already all was fading, waves and particles, there could be no things but nameless things, no

20. Mercier also suggests that Beckett's work does not so much illustrate philosophical positions as use them as structural devices, a technique he may have learned from Joyce (165).

names but thingless names. I say that now, but after all what do I know now about then. (*Three* 31)

O'Brien exhibits a similar skepticism, even if his explorations of the ramifications of the failure of epistemology seem less profound and more comic than are those of Beckett. But both O'Brien and Beckett mix the comic and the tragic in their work, and Beckett's stark, minimalist parables of futility are distinguished by a fundamentally comic vision, just as O'Brien's comedy overlays a serious and sometimes dark attitude toward the human condition. Such mixtures of tragedy and comedy should come as no surprise, being quite typical of Menippean satire in general. O'Brien figures his own Menippean skepticism toward the human ability to attain absolute knowledge of the universe in parodies of the drive to attain that knowledge like his depiction of the bizarre philosopher/scientist de Selby in *The Third Policeman* and *The Dalkey Archive*. Clissmann points out that, to O'Brien

> All thought, whether religious (*The Dalkey Archive*), scientific (*The Third Policeman*) or historical (*The Hard Life*), is subject to abuses in the hands of man who misuses his language and his intellect in the pursuit of objectives which are outside his cognisance and which become nonsense when subjected to the scrutiny of his pathetic intellect. (306)

The use of bicycle imagery in both Beckett and O'Brien leads to a subversive dialogue with Cartesian epistemology, one that radically questions the ability of the human intellect to have a knowledge of the world. This dialogue thus undermines the privileging of the mind over the body that has come to be a traditional feature of Western dualistic thinking. Other thinkers have simply reversed this hierarchy, giving epistemological precedence to the body and suggesting that it is through physical experience, especially sexuality, that a privileged access to truth can be found. Such formulations include the fiction of writers like D. H. Lawrence and the emphasis on the *jouissance* of female sexuality in the psychoanalysis of Jacques Lacan, leading to a similar privileging of feminine sexuality in Lacanian-influenced feminists like Hélène Cixous and Luce Irigaray. Indeed, there are important feminist issues at stake in this whole question—if Cartesian dualism has inevitably led to a hierarchical privileging of mind over body, that movement has traditionally been reenacted in a privileging of the masculine, associated with the processes of the intellect, over the feminine, associated with the processes of the body.

O'Brien embodies this gender-based reading of Cartesian dualism quite directly in his depiction of bicycles. Because his bicycles are part human, they can have gender, and the wooden-legged narrator of *The Third Policeman* (reminiscent of Molloy riding his bicycle with stiff leg and crutches)[21] experiences a strangely amorous encounter with a "female" bicycle:

> She moved beneath me with agile sympathy in a swift, airy stride, finding smooth ways among the stony tracks, swaying and bending skilfully to match my changing attitudes, even accommodating her left pedal patiently to the awkward working of my wooden leg. (*Third* 173)

Among other things, the Cartesian ideal physical perfection of this female bicycle seems to conflate two traditional stereotypes of the feminine—the association of women with the physical, and the "opposite" (though closely related) association of women with the ideal. These twin images in turn evoke the famous virgin-whore dichotomy that so informs the attitudes toward women of Stephen Dedalus—and perhaps of Irish society in general.

It takes very little imagination to read the above passage as an idealized fantasy of sexual intercourse from a male perspective—with the man (phallic wooden leg and all) on top and in control and the woman responding smoothly to his every whim. Such a reading is even more strongly supported by an additional description a little later in the book:

> The bicycle ran truly and faultlessly beneath me, every part of her functioning with precision, her gentle saddle-springs giving unexceptionable consideration to my weight on the undulations of the road. . . . My feet pressed down with ecstasy on the willing female pedals. (*Third* 194)

The overtness of the sexual imagery here is partially a joke on the reader—among other things O'Brien is satirizing a prurient Irish imagination that seems to see sexual connotations in everything, in spite of (or, more likely, because of) the typical Irish tendency toward repression

---

21. This wooden leg seems in most of *The Third Policeman* to offer little hindrance to the narrator's physical capabilities. For example, after the brutal murder of Mathers by the narrator and his cohort Divney (a murder that resembles those committed by Moran and by Mercier and Camier, except for the important difference that it is motivated by robbery), the narrator has no apparent trouble wielding a shovel to bury the victim (*Third* 17), whereas Molloy's more serious infirmities make him unable to aid Lousse in the burial of her dog, which he accidentally killed (how else) with his bicycle (*Three* 36). But there is a hint that the disability of O'Brien's narrator may be increasing: at one point he senses that the woodenness of his leg is gradually spreading over his whole body, a process that recalls the slow decomposition of Molloy, Moran, et al. (*Third* 115).

of sexuality.[22] As Sergeant Pluck suggestively tells the narrator when he espouses his atomic theory, "there are other things connected with ladies and ladies' bicycles that I will mention to you separately some time" (*Third* 87).

But if the relationship of rider to bicycle figures the Cartesian duality of mind and body, then it follows, according to standard Western stereotypes, that it also figures the relationship between the sexes, with man playing the superior role of mind, and woman relegated to the role of unthinking physical body. By making the sexual suggestiveness of the rider-bicycle relationship overly explicit, O'Brien thus not only provides a parody of Cartesian dualism but also suggests an invidious sexual motivation for the enduring hold that dualism has had on the Western imagination.

The way this female bicycle compensates for the narrator's own physical deficiencies suggests certain additional male fantasies of deriving wholeness from women. It also contrasts with the way Molloy's bicycle fails to be so cooperative. Yet, Molloy's clumsy and halting efforts at bicycle riding mirror the similar futility of sexual intercourse in the Beckett universe. Molloy himself shares with us his own memories of his less than satisfactory experience with coitus:

> She had a hole between her legs, oh not the bunghole I had always imagined, but a slit, and in this I put, or rather she put, my so-called virile member, not without difficulty, and I toiled and moiled until I discharged or gave up trying or was begged to stop. A mug's game in my opinion and tiring on top of that, in the long run. (*Three* 56)

In some ways the later union between Macmann and Moll in *Malone Dies* is even more grotesque, and yet the feeble efforts of these two impotent lovers take on a strangely touching sort of dignity, even grandeur, showing an impressive tenderness and courage in the face of physical disability:

> The spectacle was then offered of Macmann trying to bundle his sex into his partner's like a pillow into a pillow-slip, folding it in two, and stuffing it in with his fingers. But far from losing heart they warmed to their work. And though both were completely impotent they finally succeeded, summoning to their aid all the resources of the skin, the mucus, and the imagination, in striking from their dry and feeble clips a kind of sombre gratification. (*Three* 260)

22. O'Brien here strongly anticipates the re-reading of Victorian attitudes toward sexuality in Michel Foucault's *History of Sexuality*.

Clearly, sexual activity does not transport Beckett's characters into some transcendent realm, though sex is also not presented nearly so negatively in Beckett as some critics have claimed.[23] Beitchman notes that Beckett undercuts the Cartesian privileging of the intellect, but notes that this does not imply a

> crusade for the "rights of the flesh" as represented in our century by Henry Miller and D. H. Lawrence and in the last by Walt Whitman; for Beckett, as for Mallarmé, "the flesh is sad, alas," as sad as the intellect. (68)

Similarly, the ideal sexual intercourse in O'Brien's bicycle episode is parodic only, and the transcendence of sexuality in general is called into question in O'Brien's work. Unlike Beckett, O'Brien never presents graphic descriptions of sexual activity, though sex does frequently lurk in the margins of his texts, usually in degraded form. Representative sexual encounters in O'Brien include the rape of Sheila Lamont by Dermot Trellis in *At Swim* and the congress between Mary and Mick (and possibly Hackett) in *The Dalkey Archive*—both examples leading not to enlightenment, but to pregnancy. Indeed, in *The Poor Mouth* O'Brien's narrator (whose lack of health and vigor is reminiscent of the Beckettian hero) manages to get his wife pregnant without ever even knowing how it happened. When the baby is born, the father first thinks it is a baby pig, and by the time he realizes that it is a child, both mother and child have died. So the narrator is left alone in the rain, a sort of comic Irish Frederic Henry (*Poor* 86–87).[24]

A discussion of the feminist implications of the depiction of women and of sexuality in Beckett and O'Brien is beyond the scope of this book, though such explorations would be valuable. A close feminist analysis of Beckett's work in particular might reveal a surprising potential for positive feminist statement, both in Beckett's depiction of women and of gender and in his subversion of the kinds of authoritarian ideologies as-

---

23. Fletcher's view is typical (but, I think, incomplete): "Along with Swift, Beckett feels a fundamental disgust for the physical. Sex is a grotesque act that affords little or no pleasure, but degrades the participants by betraying them into ridiculous postures and statements" (165). Yet episodes like the story of Macmann and Moll show a respect for human determination in the face of adversity that is in many ways more affirmative than the vision of O'Brien, though O'Brien ostensibly presents a lighter and more humorous depiction of human life.

24. This episode echoes not only Hemingway, but Beckett. In "First Love" the narrator similarly is unaware of his sexual encounters; he flees home when his mate begins to give birth (*First Love* 35).

sociated with patriarchal domination. Beckett's women, of which the grotesque Moll is actually quite representative, are neither ideal angels nor specimens of physical desirability, thus undercutting both of the stereotypes of the feminine addressed in O'Brien's episode of the female bicycle.[25] Beckett's more extensive and direct treatment of sexuality shows the way he typically seems to treat issues more thoughtfully and more profoundly than does O'Brien, but there is more potential in O'Brien's treatment of gender issues than might at first be obvious. O'Brien and Beckett are in fact often concerned with the same issues. Moreover, Beckett and O'Brien employ a number of similar characters, images, and techniques to explore these issues, some of which show the commonality of their Irish cultural backgrounds, but others of which show a participation in larger trends in modern Western thought.

In particular, both of these authors, who share so much, share above all a skepticism toward any mode of investigation that would present itself as having a special access to the Truth, whether that mode involve art, philosophy, sex, or anything else. It may be that O'Brien debunks human knowledge in favor of the divine, as Clissmann claims (319). But a reading of O'Brien within the context of Menippean satire shows an irreverent challenge to authority that belies the kind of humble submissiveness indicated by Clissmann. Meanwhile, Beckett's world is thoroughly secular, and in his work if there is no truth it is because there is *no* God, not because the truth is available *only* to God. In either case genuine knowledge of reality is simply beyond the reach of human inquiry; and as Arsene tells Beckett's Watt, this knowledge belongs to the realm of "the unutterable or ineffable, so that any attempt to utter or eff it is doomed to fail, doomed, doomed to fail" (*Watt* 62). Yet, despite this common recognition, both Beckett and O'Brien did continue to "utter and eff," and the inherent paradox of their ongoing attempts to express the inability to express represents a central element of their complex, dialogic writing.

25. *Murphy*'s Celia, one of Beckett's most vivid women characters, also undercuts these stereotypes by deconstructing the opposition between the ideal (represented by her heavenly name and certain of her attitudes) and the physical (represented by her status as a prostitute).

3

Sliding Signification
At Swim-Two-Birds and the Impossibility of Authorial Control

The unnamed first-person narrator of *At Swim-Two-Birds*, O'Brien's first major work, begins his narration in a mode that indicates the polyphonic multiplicity of the entire text. Having placed in his mouth "sufficient bread for three minutes' chewing," this narrator begins a meditation on how to begin a book, concluding that a book should preferably have multiple beginnings. "A good book," he tells us, "may have three openings entirely dissimilar and inter-related only in the prescience of the author" (9). He then proceeds in the next couple of pages to give us an example of such a triple beginning, presenting an opening featuring the "Pooka McPhellimey" (a sort of folk devil), another one featuring "Mr. John Furriskey" (who appears to be an ordinary mortal—except that he was born fully-formed at age twenty-five), and a third one featuring the legendary giant Finn McCool from the realm of Irish mythology. This emphasis on the number three will recur many times in the text, which also has three conclusions, the third and final one featuring the story of a "poor German" who was obsessed with triads and who ended his life by cutting his jugular with a razor three times and leaving a suicide note with the triple farewell (which also ends O'Brien's book): "good-bye, good-bye, good-bye" (316).

The potential allegorical indications of the various threes in *At Swim* are numerous, including most obviously the central significance of the Holy Trinity to Catholicism. In this respect, O'Brien has numerous predecessors in the Catholic tradition, and one thinks immediately of the central significance of the number three to Dante's *Commedia*. O'Brien himself was also a sort of trinity, containing in his one person the separate "identities" of Flann O'Brien (a figure from the realm of "literature"), Brian O'Nolan (a "real-world" Irishman), and Myles na gCopaleen (a figure from popular culture). Indeed, the different realms in which O'Brien's different identities moved point toward the multiplicity of discourses that make up the fabric of *At Swim*. *At Swim* is first and foremost a book about other books. The base plot of the book concerns an unnamed narrator, who is himself writing a book. The narrator's book, meanwhile, features the story of Dermot Trellis, another writer. And the book Trellis is writing involves numerous characters "borrowed" from other texts, including the Western novels of William Tracy, Irish myth (Finn and his stories of the mad king Sweeny), and Irish folklore (the Pooka and the Good Fairy). Meanwhile, O'Brien's text also includes a number of brief extracts from texts encountered by his narrator, including selections from a Christian Brothers "Literary Reader," the encyclopedic *Conspectus of the Arts and Natural Sciences,* the *Concise Oxford Dictionary,* and *The Athenian Oracle.* Finally, *At Swim* includes miscellaneous fragments such as letters received by the narrator and poems written by Sweeny or by the working man's poet Jem Casey. All in all, Anne Clissmann counts a total of forty-two textual extracts within *At Swim,* combined with a total of thirty-six different styles (86), and though such counts require a certain amount of subjective judgment, it is clear that the book is a complex, multistylistic collage of fragments from a variety of different cultural domains.

In fact, *At Swim* is constructed very much according to the method recommended by the book's narrator in his exposition on the modern novel. Noting that "the novel should be a self-evident sham to which the reader could regulate at will the degree of his credulity" (33), he offers the following advice to other would-be authors of modern literary works:

> The entire corpus of existing literature should be regarded as a limbo from which discerning authors could draw their characters as required, creating only when they failed to find a suitable existing puppet. The modern novel should be largely a work of reference. Most authors spend their time saying what has been said before—usually said much better. A wealth of references to existing works would acquaint the reader instantaneously with the nature of each character, would obviate tiresome explanations and would effectively preclude mountebanks, upstarts, thimbleriggers and persons of inferior education from an understanding of contemporary literature. (33)

Such expositions on aesthetics are only one of the numerous ways in which this narrator serves as a kind of parody of Joyce's Stephen Dedalus, and it is not insignificant that the narrator's friend Brinsley (playing Lynch to the narrator's Stephen) immediately ironizes this statement with his response of "That is all my bum."[1] Indeed, numerous commentators have noted the wealth of allusions to Joyce in *At Swim*, and the bricolage technique of composition described in the above passage is very similar to the one used by Joyce throughout his career.

Despite the numerous critical discussions of O'Brien's parodies of Joyce, O'Brien's similarities to Joyce in some ways suggest that it may not be strictly *possible* to parody Joyce in the usual sense. A parody should differ from the original in such a way as to initiate a transformative dialogue with the target text, making the reader see that text in a new way. But Joyce's work always already parodies itself, so that any attempt to produce a parody of Joyce can at best produce a fairly authentic replica. There is, of course, an element of parody in O'Brien's narrator's description of modern writing, but the principal object of that parody would appear to be O'Brien's own text. So once again O'Brien reproduces Joyce's technique (self-parody), rather than parodying it.

In both Joyce and O'Brien the consistent tone of self-parody creates an extremely complex and duplicitous rhetorical texture. Both authors consistently parody various discourses of authority (science, philosophy, religion) even as they parody themselves. As a result their parodies of authoritarian discourses at the same time potentially offer themselves as parodies of *parodies,* the targets being not only the authorities directly indicated but those who would oppose those authorities in blind or simplistic ways. Joyce's texts are no doubt richer in this sense than O'Brien's, as they include a much more diverse mixture of voices in this complex effect. But there is a way O'Brien's texts go beyond Joyce's by including Joyce as one of the authorities being parodied. Thus, if Joyce is writing parodies of parodies, then O'Brien's dialogue with Joyce results in parodies of parodies of parodies. However, this layering of parodies cannot go on indefinitely before it starts to collapse. One might even argue that the ability of Joyce's work to elude parody was one of the things that O'Brien found so maddening about it—and one of the reasons why O'Brien swerved from the Joycean way in his later work. But in a surprising number of cases (and certainly in the case of *At Swim-Two-Birds*), Joyce's technique provides an excellent gloss on O'Brien's.

---

1. Niall Sheridan notes that the "self-evident sham" passage was the only portion marked in Joyce's presentation copy of *At Swim* (61). Joyce reportedly admired the book a great deal.

In particular, Joyce's work is widely acknowledged to exemplify Bakhtin's theory of the novel, so that a link between O'Brien and Joyce suggests a link between O'Brien and Bakhtin as well. Bakhtin argues that the "*auto-criticism of discourse* is one of the primary distinguishing features of the novel as a genre" (*Dialogic* 412, his emphasis). Further, he goes on to discuss different forms that this auto-criticism might take, including a type that "introduces an author who is in the process of writing the novel" (413).[2] O'Brien's self-parodic author novel, then, becomes paradigmatic of what Bakhtin terms the "Second Line" novel—a line of novels in the tradition of Menippean satire—and it is noteworthy that Bakhtin places such metafictional texts at the very center of the process through which novels interrogate the various languages and discourse structures that constitute the contemporary social and historical moment in which they are produced.[3]

I have elsewhere focused on the Menippean elements of Joyce's work in terms of what I called "sliding signification."[4] Because of the complex mixture of styles and voices, because of the denial of Aristotelian logic, because of the understanding of the fundamentally polysemic nature of language in Joyce's texts, meaning is generated on many levels and in many directions at once. Readers tend, in an effort to achieve coherence, to focus at a given time on one level and one direction of meaning, but this focus tends to be highly unstable, and meaning frequently changes direction or slides from one level to another. This sliding signification occurs at the level of individual words, as in Joyce's frequent use of the multiple signification of puns, but it also inheres in virtually every aspect of Joyce's signifying practice. Thus, Leopold Bloom may at once be an ordinary Dubliner in 1904, a reminder of Charles Stewart Parnell, a reinscription of the mythical Ulysses, a figure of Christ, and a universal figure of Everyman, with the complexity of such multiple meanings being further complicated by the ironic and self-parodic presentation of each.

The Menippean energies of *At Swim-Two-Birds* can also be usefully understood in terms of sliding signification. For example, (as the "Keats and Chapman" segments of his *Irish Times* columns indicate) O'Brien is

2. Also note Alastair Fowler's suggestion that "the most outstanding fictional genre of recent decades has surely been the poioumenon, or work-in-progress novel—the narrative of the making of a work of art" (294).

3. *At Swim* has also been placed in the tradition of Second Line texts by numerous critics. For example, Mellamphy compares the book to *The Anatomy of Melancholy, Tristram Shandy, Ulysses,* and *Finnegans Wake* (141). Sterne's *Tristram Shandy* (Frye's preferred example of Menippean satire) has been mentioned especially frequently as a predecessor of O'Brien's text. See Imhof for a detailed comparison of Sterne and O'Brien.

4. See *Joyce, Bakhtin, and the Literary Tradition.*

as much given to punning as Joyce.[5] *At Swim* contains numerous puns, some as obvious as those in "Keats and Chapman," but it employs punning in more sophisticated ways as well. The narrator at one point describes the various "cultural societies" at his Dublin college (presumably UCD), noting that "[s]ome were devoted to English letters, some to Irish letters and some to the study and advancement of the French language" (66). He thus avoids the expected pun (used several times by Joyce) involving "French letters," but at the same time evokes this pun by its very exclusion, thereby producing a sliding signification effect that moves beyond the borders of the text itself. An even more subtle punning effect occurs near the end of *At Swim,* when Dermot Trellis heads up a stairway directly behind a young servant girl, the stays in whose skirt obscure the "aesthetic" potential of the view: "Ars est celare artem, muttered Trellis, doubtful as to whether he had made a pun" (314). Trellis (or at least O'Brien) has made a pun indeed, and a double one at that—not only does he reproduce the arse/art pun that is at least as old as Chaucer's *Summoner's Tale,* but the original Latin phrase already contains an embedded pun, because *celare* (to hide) resonates with *caelare* (to engrave, i.e., to make obvious).[6] Thus, art simultaneously involves both a hiding and a declaration of art, as O'Brien demonstrates by employing a subtle pun, then explicitly calling attention to it.

The multiplicity inherent in O'Brien's puns occurs at the larger structural level of *At Swim* as well, and the book's multiple beginnings point toward a structural multiplicity that runs throughout the language of the text. The bricolage construction of the book also contributes to this effect, with the various styles and excerpts creating a complex chorus of textual voices that freely slide from one discourse to another. As Bakhtin has noted, the very presence of multiple styles in the same text creates a dialogic relationship among those styles (*Speech* 112). In *At Swim* this dialogism is further enhanced by the fact that the styles sometimes overlap and spill over into each other, as when the wag Brinsley employs the epic Finn style to describe the contemporary writer Trellis (35). This effect is itself highly Joycean, and Joyce's own voice is added to this chorus through the many allusions to his work. The motif of appropriation of material from other texts that runs throughout *At Swim* acts to destabilize normal textual boundaries and to emphasize that texts always generate meaning in dialogue with other texts—a dialogue that inevita-

---

5. Representative examples of the "Keats and Chapman" sketches can be found in *The Best of Myles* (180–200).

6. See Ahl for a useful discussion of this Latin pun (39).

bly exceeds authorial control. O'Brien also follows Joyce in *At Swim* by eschewing the use of quotation marks, thus effecting a leveling of discourses and breaking down the normal hierarchical distinction between narration and quoted speech in his text. The lack of such traditional hierarchies enhances the sliding signification effect by removing a normal source of textual stability. O'Brien also undermines normal textual hierarchies in his division of the text into various sections, each with its own italicized heading. One expects the various levels of narration in the text (the narrator's story of his own experiences, the narrator's text, Trellis's text within the narrator's text) to be nested; yet, the headings of each level are identical in style, indicating no such nesting. Further, there are many segments of the text that are clearly subsections within larger sections, but the subheadings of these subsections are given in the same style as the headings of the sections themselves.

The different plot lines and ontological levels of *At Swim* overlap and freely intermix, with characters moving easily among different texts and discourses. For example, Trellis borrows his characters from a diverse array of sources, causing characters from seemingly incompatible spheres to be thrust together in the same text. The resulting cultural mixtures create some interesting dialogic effects. In one scene of the narrator's novel, the Pooka McPhellimey (roughly representing the physical aspects of life and presumably evil) and his antithesis the Good Fairy (representing the mental and spiritual aspects of life) travel across the countryside toward the Red Swan Hotel where Trellis's character Sheila Lamont is about to give birth to a son, fathered by Trellis who endowed her with such overwhelming beauty that he raped her in a fit of passion the moment she was created. On the way they encounter and are joined by several other characters, including the cowboys Slug Willard and Shorty Andrews (characters from Tracy's books), the folksy poet Jem Casey, and the mythical Irish king Sweeny. The resulting pilgrimage is thus composed of a mixture the heteroglossia of which would have done even Chaucer proud.

In another scene Trellis's characters Paul Shanahan, John Furriskey, Antony Lamont, and Finn MacCool all converse in a room in the Red Swan while Trellis sleeps. Furriskey was created by Trellis to be the embodiment of evil, and Lamont was "hired" by Trellis to be Furriskey's nemesis. Shanahan, a professional "bit" character, has been "hired" by Trellis to perform miscellaneous minor functions. Yet, the enemies Furriskey and Lamont get along well in this scene, while the minor character Shanahan turns out to be more important than either of these major characters. The mighty Finn, meanwhile, is largely ignored by the other characters, who regard him as an old crackpot. Finn—off in his own world—begins to relate the mythical story of the mad king Sweeny, a story which is roughly translated by O'Brien from the Gaelic of the medieval Irish romance *Buile Shuibne*. Meanwhile, Shanahan tells the story of Jem Casey, "the poet of the people" (102).

The resulting counterpoint of narratives sets up a cultural dialogue between the Irish mythical past and the more prosaic present, as especially figured by the contrast between Sweeny's lyrical lays and Casey's prosaic poem in praise of "a pint of plain." P. L. Henry suggests that this contrast highlights "the cultural gap between an audience appropriate to the Middle-Irish tale and the modern doggerel-loving Dubliners" (40). Indeed, there is a temptation to read this "cultural gap" as an indication of the degraded state of modern Irish culture in relation to the glories of the mythical past, somewhat along the lines of T. S. Eliot's *Waste Land*, or of Eliot's interpretation of Joyce's use of the "mythic method" in *Ulysses*. As Clissmann puts it, "Shanahan and his companions are shown to be typical of modern Ireland, which is escapist and whose sensibilities are so atrophied that it can no longer respond to the 'grand old stuff of the native land'" (133).

Clissmann further suggests certain specifically linguistic aspects to O'Brien's critique of modern Irish culture. There is, for example, a great deal of empty talk on the part of O'Brien's Dublin characters. One of the features of O'Brien's *Irish Times* columns was "The Myles na gCopaleen Catechism of Cliché," and *At Swim-Two-Birds*—like the texts of Joyce—indicates that a great deal of the talk that goes on in Dublin consists of a rather mechanical exchange of stock phrases with little real content. As Clissmann puts it, "O'Brien's Dublin is revealed as a city of useless talk, a place where the anecdote parades as criticism, where the general is forever reduced to the particular, the familiar, and consequently, the trivial" (119). This slippage from the profound to the ridiculous is itself a sort of sliding signification because language that is not anchored in any real content is free to slide about from one meaning to another.

A similar critique of language inheres in O'Brien's metafictional technique in *At Swim*. The overt textuality of the novel calls attention to its artificial construction and continually reminds the reader that the action being represented is entirely fictional. As a result, the language of the text does not yield a representation of reality but merely a demonstration of the author's dexterity with words. And if the language of a novel need not be connected to reality, then the same might be said of other language as well. Words can have a life of their own and need not depend for their sustenance upon any direct connection to reality. In short, words are radically divorced from things, signifiers from signifieds. It is, of course, this very condition that makes sliding signification (and literature) possible, but it is certainly possible to read O'Brien's text as a critique of the extent to which this widening gap has reached the point in modern Ireland of making all language hopelessly duplicitous.

The reflexivity, or "auto-criticism" of the "self-evident sham" that is *At Swim-Two-Birds* can thus be read as O'Brien's attempt to counter the sterility of a modern language that has become lifeless and banal. Bakhtin himself identifies the auto-criticism of discourse in the novel with the Russian formalist concept of the "baring of the device," which participates in the process of defamiliarization by which literary texts attempt to wrench the reader away from mechanical perceptions of reality, allowing her to see the world in new and productive ways. The comparison of modern life to life in the mythic past effected by O'Brien in *At Swim* can thus be read as an attempt to encourage readers to look at the present from new and potentially energizing perspectives. O'Brien's use of multiple styles and multiple ontological levels participates in this trend as well, reminding the reader that there are many different ways of describing and perceiving reality, as well as suggesting that language is a rich and flexible tool for the evocation of reality that need not consist of a mere stream of clichés and stereotypes.

O'Brien's appeal to the mythic past might then be seen as an appeal to a past in which language was invested with meaning in a more fundamental way. In particular, his use of the *Buile Shuibne* suggests that the link between words and things was more stable and direct in medieval times. This suggestion resonates with the historical model of language put forth by Michel Foucault in *The Order of Things*. Foucault suggests that, during the rule of the medieval episteme, words and things were connected in the direct, mystical way suggested by the Word of God. He argues that Western thinkers from the Stoics to the sixteenth century accepted a ternary model of the sign in which signifier and signified were held together by a third element, or "conjuncture" that effected a connection between words and things based on resemblance (42). Even this medieval conception of language—coming after the punishment inflicted at Babel—lacks the absolute connection between words and things of Adamic language, though Foucault does suggest that modern Hebrew still "contains, as if in the form of fragments, the marks of the original name-giving" (36). For Foucault the change to a classical episteme then involves a further shift from the Adamic language, a change (in the seventeenth century) to a binary conception of signification in which words and things are divorced and language represents—but is not mystically connected to—reality. The modern epistemé then involves a nineteenth-century shift from representation to signification in which language takes on a life of its own apart from its representative functions.[7]

Foucault does not necessarily see these changes as a gradual deterioration, but it is certainly possible to envision a theological point of view in which this continual evolution away from the original Word of God represents an ongoing decay of language that goes back at least to the Babelian confusion, if not to the original Fall. O'Brien's treatment of language in *At Swim* can in fact be usefully read within the context of medieval Catholic meditations on the linguistic implications of the fallen state of humanity. For example, medieval thinkers already showed a certain appreciation for what I am calling sliding signification. R. A. Shoaf thus discusses the tendency toward punning in medieval poetry as an aspect of what he refers to as "juxtology," through which medieval poets link up all sorts of diverse concepts. Importantly, these connections are made largely through the offices of language itself.

> Medieval poets . . . knew full well that language is "in charge." Juxtologists, as I like to think of them, they recognized that words yoke themselves together, and together with things, in the most unpredictable ways. . . . they understood that language exceeds man's grasp and that that's what heaven is for. (Shoaf 45)

In *De vulgari eloquentia* Dante anticipates Foucault by arguing that the original Adamic speech was Hebrew, and that this original vernacular remained the universal language until the building of the Tower of Babel, whereupon the punishment levied by God led to a proliferation of different languages, which themselves were historically changeable:

> Since man is a most unstable and changeable animal, his language cannot be lasting or constant, but must vary according to times and places as do other human things such as manners and customs, I do not think there should be any doubt that language varies with time, but rather that this should be retained as certain; for if we examine our other works, we see much more discrepancy between ourselves and our ancient fellow-citizens than between ourselves and our distant contemporaries. (24–25)

Later, in *Paradiso* XXVI, Adam relates to Dante the "true" history of language, updating Dante's earlier view in *De vulgari:*

7. See the chapter "The Prose of the World" in *The Order of Things* (17–44).

La lingua ch'io parlai fu tutta spenta
innanzi che a l'ovra inconsummabile
fosse la gente di Nembròt attenta:
    ché nullo effetto mai razïonabile,
per lo piacere uman che rinovella
seguendo il cielo, sempre fu durabile.
    Opera naturale è ch'uom favella;
ma così o così, natura lascia
poi fare a voi secondo che v'abbella. (l. 124–32)

[The tongue I spoke was all extinct before
the men of Nimrod set their minds upon
the unaccomplishable task; for never
    has any thing produced by human reason
been everlasting—following the heavens
men seek the new, they shift their predilections.
    That man should speak at all is nature's act,
but how you speak—in this tongue or that—
she leaves to you and to your preference.]

Here Adam reveals that the historicity and conventionality of human language derive directly from the results of the Fall, in fact predating the Tower of Babel. As such, this linguistic condition is a fundamental property of human existence in the world. It is God's will that language be this way, and Dante, trusting that God's will is good, complies by writing his greatest poem in his Tuscan vernacular, rather than in a Latin that supposedly provides stability against the mutability of vernacular language. Stated otherwise, if the Incarnation renders the Fall a fortunate one, then it must render the arbitrariness and mutability of vernacular language fortunate as well. Dante takes advantage of this good fortune to construct a poem the richness of which is made possible by the very polysemy of vernacular language.

Dante and the other medieval "juxtologists" can embrace the sliding signification inherent in human language because they firmly believe that God is still ultimately in charge and that divine guidance will assure that the contingencies of signification in the fallen world will in the end work out for the best. In short, they can embrace a certain distance between signifier and signified because the stabilizing element that Foucault refers to as the "conjuncture" is still there to assure that semiotic order will be maintained. One could then read O'Brien's critique of modern language in Ireland as a nostalgic lament over the fact that this divine guarantee has been lost in the modern secular world, in which case O'Brien once again appears to participate in the same kind of reactionary religious modernism as T. S. Eliot.

But Dante's celebration of polysemy and the entire tradition of the Fortunate Fall already indicate ways in which changes, even ostensible degradations, can be greeted in more than one way. It is, after all, the very instability of signification in modern language that makes a text like *At Swim-Two-Birds* possible. Granted, *At Swim* demonstrates a disjuncture between modern Irish culture and the culture of the medieval past. But the kinds of cultural dialogues that occur in the book can work both ways. Joyce, for example, set up similar dialogues, but he had absolutely no sympathy for those who would nostalgically dwell on the glories of the past, Irish or otherwise. And it seems clear that Joyce's reinscription of predecessors like Homer is largely subversive and parodic, acting to undermine the authority of the great texts of the past and to suggest that perhaps the grand old stuff of the past was never really so grand in the first place. Amidst the radically unstable sliding signification of texts like *Ulysses*—or *At Swim-Two-Birds*—many readings offer themselves. Even if O'Brien himself was as bitter about the degraded condition of modern Ireland as Clissmann indicates, the instability of a text like *At Swim* allows it to escape the constraints of authorial intent, even to the point of suggesting meanings diametrically opposed to those intended by O'Brien himself.

I have argued elsewhere that when Eliot suggests that Joyce uses the authority of Homer to stabilize and add structure to his text amidst the chaos of modern civilization, he fails to appreciate the true richness of Joyce's complex signifying practice.[8] For example, the link between Leopold Bloom and Homer's Odysseus is invested with so much irony that it seems impossible to interpret the significance of that link in any nonproblematic way. Moreover, Bloom is not merely a figure of Ulysses; he is related to various other personages as well. It is, in fact, typical of Joyce's practice of sliding signification that any textual entity (not only words, but characters, setting, plot, and so on) can take on a variety of different meanings, slipping liquidly from one to another depending on the reader's focus of the moment.

The instability of character identities in *Finnegans Wake* is even more radical than in *Ulysses*, with HCE sliding among a variety of figures, including the landscape of Dublin and the same Finn MacCool used by O'Brien in *At Swim-Two-Birds*. Indeed, Finn may be a particularly apt figure to use for such purposes. O'Brien produces similar examples of

8. See *Joyce, Bakhtin, and the Literary Tradition*.

multiple figuration, indicating a source for this technique in Irish myth by having Finn declare his own multiplicity:

> I am an Ulsterman, A Connactman, A Greek, said Finn.
> I am an Ulsterman, a Connactman, a Greek, said Finn.
> I am Cuchulainn, I am Patrick.
> I am Carbery-Cathead, I am Goll.
> I am my own father and my son.
> I am every hero from the crack of time. (24)

O'Brien's Dermot Trellis functions as a similar emblem of multiple figuration. For example, within the context of *At Swim* the torments and trial that Trellis undergoes late in *At Swim* clearly echo the experiences of Sweeny as narrated by Finn earlier in the book. But the suffering of Trellis also recalls the tribulations of Bloom in the "Circe" chapter of *Ulysses*. Meanwhile, Bloom in "Circe" already echoes both Christ and Parnell, leading to an association of Trellis with these figures as well. Trellis (whose very name suggests "cross") is linked to Christ at several points in *At Swim*. But the domineering Trellis is even more strongly reminiscent of Stephen Dedalus's God-like artist, providing a link between Trellis and God Himself, a link that potentially provides some of the book's most trenchant satire. Trellis's practices of artistic creation—especially his theory of aestho-autogamy—clearly echo the Creation of God. In particular, the practice of aestho-autogamy allows Trellis to create "living" characters "from an operation involving neither fertilization nor conception" (55), in what might be read as a parody of the Virgin Birth so central to Catholicism.

The "press extract" describing the birth of John Furriskey by aestho-autogamy provides details that make this parodic reading even more available:

> For fully five centuries in all parts of the world epileptic slavies have been pleading it in extenuation of uncalled-for fecundity. It is a very familiar phenomenon in literature. The elimination of conception and pregnancy, however, or the reduction of these processes to the same mysterious abstraction as that of the paternal factor in the commonplace case of unexplained maternity, has been the dream of every practicing psycho-eugenist the world over. (55)

In short, this extract hints—despite the careful claim that the phenomenon is only five centuries old—at the extremely subversive notion that mysterious events of which the Virgin Birth is the prototype are commonly used as an excuse for illegitimate pregnancies. This link between aestho-autogamy and the Immaculate Conception also has the effect of making the supposedly evil Furriskey—a product of aestho-autogamy—a figure of Christ.

Such parodies of Catholicism are familiar in the work of the apostate Joyce, though they might come as a surprise in the work of O'Brien, who apparently remained a believing Catholic throughout his life. Of course, one could argue that O'Brien's faith in Catholicism is strong enough that he feels assured that the dialogues he sets up between the creations of modern writers and the Creation of God will work entirely to the benefit of the latter, suggesting that the productions of the former are hopelessly degraded in comparison. But again, once such dialogues are set in motion, O'Brien is unable to control the eventual implications of those dialogues for specific readers. And O'Brien goes out of his way to emphasize the motif, including it (appropriately enough) three times in the text. Later, when the Good Fairy attempts to assure the Pooka that he need not fear any carnal interest on the part of the Fairy in the Pooka's wife, he does so in terms that again clearly suggest the conception of Christ:

> Even if it were desirable, replied the Good Fairy, angelic or spiritual carnality is not easy and in any case the offspring would be severely handicapped by being half flesh and half spirit, a very baffling and neutralizing assortment of fractions since the two elements are forever at variance. (149)

Still later, a third reinscription of the birth of Christ occurs in the birth of Orlick Trellis, who is half human and half fictional character. O'Brien's narrator notes the difficulty of depicting such a character. He considers giving Orlick only half a body, but decides that such a solution would introduce insurmountable technical difficulties and therefore decides to make him appear outwardly human (206–7). Orlick, too, becomes a figure of Christ, which is appropriate given that he is the son of the God-figure Dermot Trellis.

The way Orlick Trellis and Christ both straddle ontological boundaries is emblematic of the ontological instability of *At Swim-Two-Birds* as a whole. And if this instability can lead to the kind of sliding signification that allows readings that run directly contrary to authorial intention, O'Brien appears to anticipate that possibility in the plot of *At Swim*. Dermot Trellis is a domineering author figure who demands complete control of his texts, and as such he maintains a tyrannical power over his characters. However, when Trellis sleeps his characters are free to act on their own. Not only do they evade Trellis's intentions during these periods (as when Furriskey falls in love with and marries the slavey Peggy, rather than brutally raping her as he was intended by Trellis to do), but they even instigate a rebellion designed to end in the overthrow and death of Trellis, thus freeing them once and for all.

The characters enlist Orlick in this effort, and in a startling reversal of the normal ontological priority of authors over characters they induce Orlick to write a book in which his father Dermot is the main character. Meanwhile, Shanahan, Furriskey, and Lamont all contribute ideas as Orlick constructs a tale in which the Pooka subjects Trellis to a variety of horrid tortures then drags him to a court where he undergoes a surrealistic trial. The plan is to have Trellis condemned to death and executed, though this plan does cause a certain amount of ontological anxiety on the part of the characters, who wonder if they will continue to exist if the author who created them is destroyed through their efforts. "I don't think the like of this has been done before, you know," warns Orlick (301).

The like has perhaps been attempted once before, however—if Trellis is a figure of God, then this move echoes the rebellion of Satan and his angels against God's rule in heaven, making Orlick (like Joyce's Stephen Dedalus) a figure of both Christ and Satan. The rebellion in heaven failed, of course, and the rebellion in *At Swim-Two-Birds* fails as well. Just as the trial is about to reach its climax in Orlick's text, Trellis is saved by an incursion from his own ontological level when his servant Teresa accidentally burns the part of his manuscript in which Shanahan, Furriskey, and the other characters who are plotting against him were created. In short, these rebellious characters (like Satan and his rebellious angels) are cast into the fire. Trellis, however, is saved not by his own God-like powers, but by pure accident, further emphasizing the impossibility of the authorial control he so desperately seeks. It may be important that the characters cease to exist when the manuscript is burned, even as their creator continues to live, the implication being that texts, once written, have an existence of their own independent of authorial control. Indeed, this existence is even harder to control than this motif indicates, as Shanahan et alii do in fact still exist in the pages of *At Swim-Two-Birds*. It may be that authors can burn manuscripts, but once a book is in print its existence escapes the dominion of its author entirely. Fictional characters may exist only on paper, but paper may be a rather more durable medium than it at first appears to be.

Trellis's authoritarian domination of his characters and their subsequent revolt initiates an interrogation of literature as a locus of both authoritarian and emancipatory energies. As with Joyce, the technique of sliding signification has a number of possible social and political implications. All of these implications are, however, inherently ambiguous because of the very nature of this signification process. Virtually no aspect of *At Swim-Two-Birds* lends itself to the determination of a definitive reading. The dialogue between modern and medieval Irish culture might be taken to indicate that modern culture is hopelessly degraded relative to its grand ancestry, or it might be read to suggest that this grand past is irrelevant and that a nostalgic longing for it is silly at best. It may be true that modern Dubliners like Furriskey and Shanahan show no respect for the mythic past as represented by Finn, but it is also true that Finn himself is a dreamy figure, disengaged from reality and unable to escape the solipsistic world of his own storytelling.

Such inherent ambiguities place O'Brien in very much the same position as his creature Trellis—always in danger that his text will revolt in the hands of readers, producing meanings far beyond, or even directly contrary to the author's original intention. Even the plot of the book is ultimately uncontrollable, and it is not surprising that O'Brien is forced to resort to the expedient of the burned manuscript to escape from the vertiginous swirl of paradox and confusion brought about by the mixture of ontological levels in his text. Amidst the sliding signification of *At Swim*, words can take on multiple meanings, characters can become figures of a variety of personages, and intertextual connections can lead in numerous directions. Which of these multiple possibilities will in fact be engaged by a given reader depends in large part upon the particular perspective and cultural background of that reader, factors which are clearly beyond authorial control.

Because of the inherent ambiguity of the text, *At Swim* offers itself to a wide variety of interpretations, depending on the perspective and strategy that the reader brings to the text. For example, should one choose to take a Marxist point view, the sliding signification of *At Swim* can be read as a demonstration that language itself has become commodified in capitalist society. It is, after all, a central characteristic of the commodity that boundaries and differences are effaced, reducing all commodities to interchangeability. Much of Joyce's work clearly functions as a critique of modern bourgeois society, so this reading of sliding signification as commodification can be highly useful in his case. *At Swim-Two-Birds* addresses the phenomenon of commodification as well. For one thing, the textual apparatus of the book shows a clear awareness of the physical nature of the medium, as in the use of italicized section headings. The motif of lost and destroyed manuscript pages that runs throughout the text emphasizes the materiality of writing as well. José Lanters suggests that "[w]hat makes *At Swim* special in its treatment of literary conventions is that it deals with the very ingredients of the novel as tangible objects" (271). And the narrator's theory of constructing texts from fragments of other texts tends to convert authorship into a process of mass production.[9] He notes that his theory is intended to help authors to "make big money" a notion that resides in the narrator's pun "to make a book," which encompasses both this automated process of book production and the motif of betting on horses (32).[10]

This conflation of the process of authorship as mystical creation with the prosaic activity of manufacturing recurs in *At Swim* several times. For example, in the work of the hack poet Jem Casey, the writing of poetry is related to the digging of holes; and Casey can simultaneously dig with his pick and compose, workmanlike, a poem "a yard long" in his head (102–3). This conversion of creation into production tends to make commodities even of human beings. In Shanahan's story of his days as a character in William Tracy's Westerns, a group of black maids are rustled along with a herd of cattle, the two thefts being considered to be very much of the same order, as Shanahan's reaction shows: "I'm not what you call fussy when it comes to women but damn it all I draw the line when it comes to carrying off a bunch of black niggers—human beings, you must remember—and a couple of thousand steers, by God" (76). Similarly, a "press extract" in the text quotes Tracy's Swiftian meditation on the social advantages that would accrue from the development of techniques for delivering offspring fully grown, thus saving the expense and trouble of child rearing. The business opportunities associated with this ability "would transform matrimony from the sordid struggle that it often is to an adventurous business enterprise of limitless possibilities" (56). And this conversion of the miracle of human conception into mere factory-like production is even more overt when Brinsley observes of the slavey Teresa (created by the narrator to serve Dermot Trellis) that such servants "were the Ford cars of humanity; they were created to a standard pattern by the hundred thousand" (43).

Clearly, there is a great deal of social satire in this motif, which suggests that individuals (especially women, minorities, and manual workers) in modern bourgeois society have been converted into commodities,

9. *At Swim*, in fact, grows out of O'Brien's own earlier project to develop the "Ready-Made" novel that would allow mass production of texts to exploit the increased reading audience brought about by compulsory education. See Sheridan (41–44).

10. Similarly, when the narrator borrows money from his uncle to buy a book that he needs for school, he winds up spending this "book-money" to bet on a horse (51). Significantly, the book he was to buy—Heine's *Die Harzreise*—is a satire of philistinism.

mere artifacts of the economic system. But O'Brien's dialogue with commodification can be read in different ways. One might, for example, interpret his use of commodified language and treatment of people as commodities either as symptoms of the arrant commodification of modern society in general or as critiques of that commodification. Such ambiguities again emphasize the importance of reading the text from a clear interpretative perspective—and of realizing that one is doing so. Most readings of *At Swim-Two-Birds* have been conservative, suggesting that the book is a critique of the fallen condition of modern Irish society that is not worthy of the rich past of Irish myth and folklore. Such readings may indeed be consistent with O'Brien's own ideology, but they are in no way necessitated by the text itself. If one reads *At Swim* within the tradition of Menippean satire, the polyphony of styles, discourses, and ontological levels becomes invested with carnivalesque energies that can make the book a strong antiauthoritarian statement. The multiplicity of language in *At Swim* amply illustrates Bakhtin's concept of dialogic discourse, a concept which implies that there is something in the property of language itself that tends to work against the imposition of narrow, authoritarian, monologic points of view.

Bakhtin's notion of the dialogic nature of all discourse implies that no single group or attitude can ever dominate language entirely. In every society there will be a dominant discourse (actually, a family of discourses), but that discourse can only define itself in relation to other repressed discourses with which it maintains a dialogic tension. Thus, the very nature of language indicates that there will always be a possibility that opposing voices can arise, even if they must do so through parodic manipulation of the language of authority. Bakhtin sees language as a powerful political weapon, but it is a weapon that is inherently a two-edged sword—it may serve as a means of oppression, but it serves at the same time as a means of liberation. As Patricia Yaeger notes, emphasizing the importance of Bakhtin for an understanding of the subversive possibilities of women's discourse:

> Any dominant discourse is inherently flawed, for it can only come into dominance by repressing other discourses . . . . Discourse is, then, an arena of permanent struggle in which any language that seems "unitary" is always embattled. (255)

A similar struggle is at work in *At Swim-Two-Birds* in its various dialogues between the past and the present, popular and "high" culture, authorial intention and textual multiplicity. It is, in fact, through the prominence of such dialogism in the text that *At Swim* is most reminiscent of Joyce. And one might even see in this very parallel a potential explanation for O'Brien's later turn away from Joycean writing practice. For Joyce, the ability of language to exceed any conventional notion of authorial intention seems to have been greeted with celebration because it offered exciting new possibilities for the generation of meanings. For Joyce, the more meanings the better; but this open acceptance of the sliding signification inherent in language runs directly contrary to all theological conceptions of language, and particularly to Catholicism. O'Brien himself expressed open contempt for the arrogance of would-be God-like controlling authors, but it may well be that the exploration in *At Swim-Two-Birds* of the implications of such linguistic multiplicity led the Catholic O'Brien to some rather terrifying conclusions, from which he then backed away in his later work.

If one again compares O'Brien to Dante, the condition in which O'Brien finds the language of modernism might be directly compared to the degraded kind of language that Dante encounters in hell. Dante's pilgrimage and spiritual purification in the *Commedia* consist very much of a journey through and purification of language. Similarly, O'Brien's demonstration of the inappropriateness of allusions to the Irish mythic past in his modern Dublin parallels the way past writings (especially Dante's own) are continually misused in the *Inferno*. As Teodolinda Barolini points out, "Textually, the governing principle of the *Inferno* is misuse, which is objectified into a series of misquotations operating at all levels of textual activity" (4). Words in the *Inferno* are inherently duplicitous, and the danger of linguistic deception and misrepresentation is ever present. By the time of the *Paradiso*, however, allusions are invariably appropriate, and quotations are invariably accurate—language is once again the language of Truth, guaranteed by God. In *At Swim-Two-Birds* it may be that O'Brien discovers a modern world in which this guarantee no longer holds. Under these conditions he is unable to follow Dante on the road to a heavenly language. Instead, he proceeds, in his next book, on a descent into hell.

On the other hand, one should always observe caution in jumping to conclusions about O'Brien's complex, duplicitous texts. It may be true that in *At Swim-Two-Birds* O'Brien discovers the impossibility of ultimate authorial control, and it may also be true that he found this discovery unnerving in some ways. But one should keep in mind that O'Brien consistently mocks the pretensions of would-be controlling authors (of whom he seems to have regarded Joyce as the embodiment) throughout his work. *At Swim-Two-Birds* reveals that authors can never be assured of achieving their intended goals; but that, paradoxically enough, may have been precisely what O'Brien intended to do.

4

The Impossibility of Knowledge
Science, Philosophy, and *The Third Policeman*

In *Problems of Dostoevsky's Poetics* Bakhtin argues that Menippean satire frequently employs fantastic imagery and situations in order to create extraordinary situations for the testing of philosophical ideas. He emphasizes that "the fantastic here serves not for the positive *embodiment* of truth, but as a mode for searching after truth, provoking it, and most important, *testing* it" (114, Bakhtin's emphasis). This philosophical (and especially epistemological) element of Menippean satire occurs frequently in O'Brien's work, but it figures most prominently in *The Third Policeman,* which is above all else a detailed exploration (and deflation) of traditional Western epistemological systems like science, philosophy, and religion.

O'Brien's epistemological skepticism has an extensive background in modern philosophy. In 1873 a youthful Friedrich Nietzsche wrote a little essay entitled "On Truth and Lies in the Nonmoral Sense." The essay was never published in Nietzsche's lifetime and was never even finished—it comes down to us in the form of two completed sections and preliminary notes toward several more. The essay deals, more or less, with the question of human knowing and especially with the fundamental role that language plays in the conceptualization of all knowledge.

> It is this way with all of us concerning language: we believe that we know something about the things themselves when we speak of trees, colors, snow, and flowers; and yet we possess nothing but metaphors for things—metaphors which correspond in no way to the original entities. . . . Thus the genesis of language does not proceed logically in any

case, and all the material within which the man of truth, the scientist, and the philosopher later work and build, if not derived from never-never land, is at least not derived from the essence of things. (82–83; sec. 1)[1]

To Nietzsche, all knowledge is indirect and metaphorical and "reality" is nothing but "an X which remains inaccessible and undefinable for us" (83; sec. 1). Language does not refer to some external reality, but only to itself, and the same can be said for all knowledge. Any link between language and reality is purely metaphorical. "Every concept arises from the equation of unequal things," Nietzsche writes (83; sec. 1). All knowledge arises in relation to other knowledge, and the resultant epistemological self-referentiality results in an infinite regression that can never hit bottom.

Nietzsche's essay suggests that the search for Truth and the quest for centers and origins that underlie the epistemological investigations of post-Cartesian Western philosophy are ultimately doomed to failure. This suggestion strongly anticipates many of the proclamations of recent poststructuralist philosophers like Jacques Derrida—and with good reason. As Sanford Schwartz points out, the "On Truth" essay has become a sort of "manifesto" of the poststructuralist movement (75). Nietzsche's radical questioning of the ultimate authenticity of all human knowledge also bears surprising similarities to certain developments in modern science and resonates with many later developments in literature, where numerous authors have launched similar demystifying assaults against the epistemological tradition of the Enlightenment. Such assaults have formed a major part of the projects of many modern writers, playing an especially important role in the work of Irish writers like Joyce and Beckett, who react against the Berkeleyan tradition in Irish thought. One of the most effective of these Irish antiepistemological texts is O'Brien's relatively obscure *The Third Policeman*.

Like Nietzsche's "On Truth" essay (and equally appropriately, given that both works question the possibility of closure and completion), O'Brien's novel was not published during the author's lifetime. The book is a highly carnivalesque deflation of epistemological pretensions. And, echoing Bakhtin's emphasis in *Rabelais and His World* that depictions of the underworld are traditionally a strong locus of carnivalesque imagery in literature, *The Third Policeman* features a bizarre Kafkaesque after-

1. For the reader's convenience all references to the works of Nietzsche are given by both page number (first) and section number, because the latter do not vary among the many available editions of Nietzsche's work.

world in which a nameless narrator stumbles upon a surrealistic police station. Here he meets Policeman MacCruiskeen and Sergeant Pluck and learns that they have a mysterious third colleague as well, the enigmatic Policeman Fox. Marginal though this enigmatic third policeman may appear to most of the action of O'Brien's novel, it is highly appropriate that he be the title character. The book is largely about the confident pretensions of Cartesian epistemology to be able to reach (and recognize) Truth, and the mysterious and inaccessible Fox serves as a personification of an equally elusive Truth.[2]

Reading *The Third Policeman* in conjunction with philosophical projects like Nietzsche's helps to bring into focus many important aspects of the book. For one thing, such comparisons emphasize that *The Third Policeman* is very much a novel of ideas, despite O'Brien's own claim in a letter to William Saroyan that "[t]he only good thing about it is the plot."[3] And the way the book challenges and indicates the folly of a number of modern scientific and philosophical notions again points toward O'Brien's important participation in the tradition of Menippean satire. Further, Nietzsche's expression of epistemological futility deals centrally with language and with the fundamentally mediated and metaphorical nature of all linguistic representations of reality. Reading O'Brien through Nietzsche's work thus suggests a similar interrogation of language in *The Third Policeman*, which runs directly counter to the common critical perception that, after *At Swim-Two-Birds*, O'Brien moves away from reflexive linguistic experiment and toward more realistic fiction.[4]

There are any number of parodies of the Western drive for knowledge sprinkled throughout *The Third Policeman*. The action of the book is set in motion by the narrator's desire to publish an edition of the collected works of a certain de Selby, whom O'Brien depicts as a comic caricature of scholars and scientists everywhere. But in order to effect this publication the narrator needs money; thus (along with his associate John Divney), he murders and robs a rich old man by the name of Mathers.[5] Divney and the narrator divest their victim of a black cashbox,

2. Fox resonates with a number of other depictions of enigma in modern literature. It is interesting, for example, that the puzzling "answer" to Stephen Dedalus's riddle in the "Nestor" chapter of *Ulysses* is "the fox burying his grandmother" (22).

3. This letter is reprinted on page 200 of the New American Library edition of the book.

4. Some critics have, indeed, challenged this common perception. Silverthorne, for example, argues that "The literary self-consciousness of *At Swim-Two-Birds* is shared to some extent by *The Third Policeman* (72).

5. When the narrator finally encounters Fox late in the book, Fox turns out to have the face of Mathers. The implication is that the narrator has not found the "true" Fox, but

which Divney then hides until things can quiet down. The narrator does not know the hiding place, however, and Divney will not tell him; consequently, for three years the narrator refuses to leave Divney's side lest the latter retrieve the loot on his own.

Finally, Divney announces that it is time to get the box, and in a parody of the quest motif in which the black box plays the part of the Holy Grail (symbolically, knowledge itself), the narrator goes for the box in the location that Divney indicates. He finds it easily, but "something happened," and after his retrieval of the box the narrative immediately veers from its heretofore realistic mode into a strange, unsettling, and surrealistic melodrama (23). An apparition of the dead Mathers appears, and from there things become increasingly bizarre. We do not learn until near the end of the book that this sudden change occurs because Divney has booby-trapped the box and that the narrator has been killed in the ensuing explosion.

In *The Third Policeman* all epistemological quests are booby-trapped, and those who would seek a final Truth are likely to meet the same unfortunate fate as the unnamed narrator. The shadowy de Selby serves as one of the central illustrations of this principle, and we are treated (especially in a series of farcical mock-scholarly footnotes) to a general introduction to de Selby's work.[6] The epitome of de Selby's evasion of epistemological inquiry occurs with the case of his "Codex," a mysterious document that is

> a collection of some two thousand sheets of foolscap closely hand-written on both sides. The signal distinction of the manuscript is that not one word of the writing is legible. Attempts made by different com-

---

has merely run up against his own preoccupations, a suggestion highly in accord with Nietzsche's critique of epistemology.

6. Irish writers, with a long tradition of parodies of pedantry, often employ such footnotes. The prototype for this technique would appear to be Swift's *Tale of a Tub*, with the "Nightlessons" section of *Finnegans Wake* serving as the most important modern reincarnation of the motif. Samuel Beckett has also used footnotes to good effect in *Watt*. Hugh Kenner presents some interesting discussions of the implications of these footnotes in Swift, Joyce, and Beckett in terms of their emphasis on the physical nature of the book as medium, an emphasis that arises from the particularly oral nature of Irish culture. See also Benstock for a general discussion of the use of footnotes in fictional texts. Benstock takes a Derridean perspective to argue that the inherently marginal nature of the footnote calls into question the general perception that texts are self-contained and complete. "To read a footnote is to be forcibly reminded of the inherent multi-textuality of all texts" (220n 2). In short, footnotes are a reminder of the futility of epistemological readings of texts because the text is not locatable as an object of study—important information always exists outside the apparent boundaries of the text.

mentators to decipher certain passages which look less formidable than others have been characterised by fantastic divergencies. (145n)[7]

This elusive "Codex" may be at least partially a parodic commentary on Joyce's *Finnegans Wake,* a text that O'Brien apparently disliked intensely.[8] Indeed, the parallel with the *Wake* becomes even stronger in the readings of one du Garbandier, who claims that this "Codex" is merely "a repository of obscene conundrums, accounts of amorous adventures and erotic speculation" (146n).[9]

There are also rumors that the "Codex" may be a forgery, and to top things off, there are at least four different copies, each radically different from all the others, that claim to be the genuine original of the document (146n). The "Codex" thus functions, like Policeman Fox, as a representation of the illusory nature of the "Truth" so fervently sought by the inquiries of Western epistemology. But even when de Selby's texts can be located and deciphered, it is still often difficult to ascertain their authenticity. The authorship of certain texts is in question, "raising issues of no less piquancy than those of the Bacon-Shakespeare controversy" (93n). And we find that one Le Fournier ("the reliable French commentator")

7. This description would appear to parody both the status of certain difficult modern texts and the critics of those texts. This motif becomes even clearer in *The Dalkey Archive,* O'Brien's later reinscription of *The Third Policeman,* in which Mick Shaughnessy rails against the excesses of Joyce critics, noting that "I've read some stupid books written *about* Joyce and his work, mostly by Americans" (112).

8. Mackenzie argues that O'Brien's alarm over the excesses of the *Wake* actually drove him away from the experimentalism of *At Swim-Two-Birds* and back toward a more realistic mode of writing in *The Third Policeman* and afterward. Mackenzie's article makes some interesting points, though, like most critics of O'Brien, he perhaps attributes to Joyce too much direct influence over O'Brien's career. See Browne for a useful discussion of the importance of a number of writers other than Joyce (including Huysmans, Huxley, James Branch Cabell, and James Stephens). Clissmann also presents useful discussions of many of these same authors (particularly Cabell, whose *Cream of the Jest* seems an especially important intertext for *At Swim-Two-Birds*) (93–95). Clissmann also points out that de Selby himself seems to be modeled on Des Esseintes, the hero of Huysmans's *Rebours,* and on Slawkenbergius, the comic scholarly authority in *Tristram Shandy.*

9. See Hart for a discussion of the import of the many scatological passages and images in the *Wake.* Hart notes: "It seems to have been a part of Joyce's design to include allusions to every possible form of sexual deviation, and to use the most common perversions as primary material" (205). Interestingly, the implied hint that du Garbandier may be indulging his own prurient fantasies in producing this interpretation seems to have been anticipated by Joyce, whose "Nightlessons" section includes a suggestion (echoing Freud's discussions of Leonardo da Vinci) that scientific research is ultimately inspired by sexual drives. Thus, the scientific theorizing of the boys Dolph and Kevin (a.k.a. Shaun and Shem) turns into a fantasy of lifting the apron of ALP to explore the secret regions of their mother's body (293–97).

has suggested that de Selby's bizarre designs for experimental housing came about because the great scientist was so absent-minded that he mistook some of his own meaningless doodles for housing plans and then attempted to develop theories to explain the drawings (21–22n).

Many of de Selby's theories appear patently ridiculous, and the great scholar seems distinguished by an unparalleled lack of any common sense whatsoever. For example, de Selby concludes, upon examining some old cinematograph films, that the flow of time is not continuous but is, in fact, "a succession of static experiences each infinitely brief" (50). The examination of these films is a piece of extremely tedious research—and no wonder. "Apparently he had examined them patiently picture by picture and imagined that they would be screened in the same way, failing at that time to grasp the principle of the cinematograph" (50).

De Selby's ruminations here may be a direct commentary on the theories of time discussed by J. W. Dunne, an important source for many of the ideas in *The Third Policeman*.[10] But the picture of de Selby painstakingly examining these strips of film frame by individual frame with no conception of the connection between frames also serves as a very effective general parody of the Western analytical drive to partition nature into manageable segments for close investigation. The motif of a division of time into an infinite number of discrete fragments obviously owes much to the paradoxes of Zeno, and the example of the film especially evokes the work of one of Zeno's prominent modern commentators, Henri Bergson. Bergson similarly points to the cinema as a metaphor for the way modern man has segmented the flow of time into discrete fragments in order to render it more amenable to analytical mastery. However, he approaches this "cinematographic illusion" with a certain ambivalence: this process of dividing time into discrete fragments forces us to be forever separated from any direct knowledge of the true flux of reality, yet it has served us well as a means of gaining at least *some* knowledge of that reality, belated and secondary though it might be. As Bergson notes, "The cinematographic method is therefore the only practical method" (333).[11]

Bergson does propose an alternative, however. He suggests that we should attempt to develop a second method of perceiving time that will evade the negative effects of the "practical," or cinematographic method:

10. See O'Toole for a useful discussion of the significance of Dunne's work in O'Brien's book.

11. The link between the cinematic imagery of O'Brien and Bergson and the situation of Zeno's paradoxes is clear, and Bergson attempts to deal with those paradoxes immediately after his discussion of the cinematograph (335–40).

> The first [cinematographic] kind of knowledge has the advantage of
> enabling us to foresee the future and of making us in some measure
> masters of events. . . . This other knowledge . . . is practically useless, it
> will not extend our empire over nature, it will even go against certain
> natural aspirations of the intellect; but, if it succeeds, it is reality itself
> that it will hold in a firm and final embrace. (372)

Bergson here apparently recommends that we eschew the attempts of
science to gain a mastery over natural phenomena and that we instead
seek a sort of mystic harmony with nature. But he gives himself away
with his description of a desire to hold reality in a "firm and final embrace": Bergson, in his own way, is also seeking mastery.

That all systematic programs for the pursuit of knowledge inevitably
lead to such invidious quests for mastery is dramatized in *The Third Policeman* not only in the hilarious scholarly bumbling of de Selby but in
that of his commentators as well. Indeed (in a trend not unknown
among contemporary literary scholars), the narrator seems to have spent
a great deal more time reading de Selby's critics than reading de Selby
himself. The narrator owns a complete set of the works of the two "principal commentators," Hatchjaw and Bassett, and has even set out to learn
French and German in order to read commentaries in those languages
(11).

The various interpretations produced by de Selby's critics (and the
various arguments that arise among them) present a parody of the narcis-
sism of scholarly commentary that rivals the hobby-horse phenomenon
of Sterne's *Tristram Shandy* or the solipsistic marginalia of Charles Kin-
bote in Nabokov's *Pale Fire*. De Selby's commentators seem to spend
more time commenting on (and generally reviling) each other than on
explicating the works of de Selby. And the depths of this cross-commen-
tary are as bottomless as those presented by de Selby's own texts. For
example, Hatchjaw and Bassett carry on a running feud with rival scholars Kraus and du Garbandier, the latter of whom generally take a much
more negative (and even obscene) view of de Selby's work. Both Hatchjaw and Bassett conclude that Kraus and du Garbandier are one and the
same, though Hatchjaw is convinced that "du Garbandier" is merely a
pseudonym sometimes used by Kraus, while Bassett believes that
"Kraus" is a sometime-pseudonym of du Garbandier (168n). But turn-
about is fair play, and when Hatchjaw sets out in search of the real
Kraus/du Garbandier, someone (apparently Kraus/du Garbandier) engineers a plot that results in Hatchjaw's arrest as an alleged impersonator
of Hatchjaw himself (171n). From there Hatchjaw's career spirals down-
ward until he winds up as an agent for a brothel in Hamburg (172n).

That Hatchjaw, Bassett, and their fellow scholars never succeed in solving any of the mysteries surrounding de Selby (or each other) is merely another manifestation of the futility of all quests for certain knowledge in *The Third Policeman*. The shenanigans of these hapless scholars are endless in more ways than one. Not only does their work fail to reach conclusions but it in turn generates additional work by meta-commentators (like Henderson, author of *Hatchjaw and Bassett*) whose work is similarly inconclusive. There is an implication that this process might spiral outward forever. The notes in *The Third Policeman* might be construed as a metametacommentary on de Selby one level above Henderson, just as the essay I am writing now can be read as a meta-metametacommentary one level above O'Brien.

This series of endlessly expanding commentaries is only one of the many manifestations of similar phenomena of Nietzschean infinite regression to be found scattered throughout O'Brien's work. The best known example of this motif in O'Brien's fiction involves the nested narratives of *At Swim-Two-Birds*, but it may be that the most striking examples appear in *The Third Policeman*.[12] De Selby's researches into the nature of time include a recognition that, because the speed of light is finite, a man looking in a mirror actually sees an image of himself as a younger man. Employing his usual scientific technique of extending a basically sound premise until it reaches absurdity, de Selby then constructs an arrangement wherein one mirror is reflected within another, leading to an infinite regression of images. Interposing his own image in this series, de Selby claims to have been able to use a telescope to trace his diminishing reflections so far back that he is finally able to see himself as a young boy, though alas he is unable to view himself in infancy due to practical problems like "the curvature of the earth and the limitations of the telescope" (65).

De Selby's theory is nonsense, of course, and his experimental results quite impossible. We in fact learn that he was apparently obsessed with mirrors in general, to the point that he refused to look at anything *except* through mirrors (64n). But Nietzsche's work suggests that we *always* see everything only through conceptual mirrors, and this episode makes a number of points that are extremely germane to O'Brien's overall critique of Western epistemology. De Selby's inability to trace his image back to

12. In recent critical discourse, such effects are often identified with the phenomenon of the *mise en abyme*, of which stories about writers who are writing stories about writers, and so forth, is the paradigmatic example. *At Swim-Two-Birds* thus provides a classic example of the effect. Several commentators have discussed this phenomenon in O'Brien, particularly as it might have been inspired by Huxley's *Point Counter Point*. See Mackenzie for a particularly cogent discussion of this point (58–59).

infancy dramatizes the incapacity of human methods of inquiry (particularly science) ever to reach the final answer to any given question. This example mirrors (so to speak) Nietzsche's comments on the indirectness of all knowledge and implies that what our researches reveal is an infinite series of reflections of reality, while Truth itself recedes from us in a sequence of deferrals until finally it drops out of sight altogether.

But what makes this commentary on science all the more meaningful is that, absurd or not, de Selby's mirror research bears some rather striking resemblances to real scientific developments of the twentieth century. In particular, the centrality of mirrors and of the speed of light to de Selby's experiment identifies it as a clear descendant of the famous Michelson-Morley experiment of the 1880s, which involved measurements of the speed of light made using a system of mirrors. Significantly, from the perspective of classical physics the results of Michelson and Morley—which showed that the speed of light was invariant regardless of other motion in the system—were just as absurd as those of de Selby. For over twenty years, physicists around the world busied themselves in elaborate attempts to explain the phenomenon, but not until Einstein's introduction of special relativity in 1905 could a satisfactory explanation be produced—and then only at the expense of jettisoning the comforting, common-sense world of Newtonian mechanics.

If de Selby's fascination with mirrors metaphorically comments upon the impossibility of a direct perception of reality, other elements of *The Third Policeman* do so even more directly. In the strange underworld land of eternity that he visits with Puck and MacCruiskeen, the narrator encounters certain objects of indeterminate color, shape, and dimension that will not respond to his habits of perception: "Simply their appearance, if even that word is not inadmissable, was not understood by the eye and was in any event indescribable" (135). And the researches of Policeman MacCruiskeen include the production of invisible objects and of inaudible music, as well as work with strange colors that elude perception: "It was not one of the colours a man carries inside his head like nothing he ever looked at with his eyes," Puck explains to the narrator about one of MacCruiskeen's inventions (154).

The objects in *The Third Policeman* that cannot be perceived in ordinary terms or described in ordinary language bear similarities to the strange phenomena observed by modern physics. Werner Heisenberg describes the difficulty of grasping the behavior of subatomic particles on the basis of everyday experience:

> The mathematically formulated laws of quantum theory show clearly that our ordinary intuitive concepts cannot be unambiguously applied

to the smallest particles. All the words or concepts we use to describe ordinary physical objects, such as position, velocity, color, size, and so on, become indefinite and problematic if we try to use them of elementary particles. (*Across* 114)

In short, if the landscape of *The Third Policeman* appears to violate many of the precepts of conventional logic, then so does the real world, especially as described in modern scientific constructions like relativity and quantum mechanics. Thus, Niels Bohr notes that the discoveries of modern physics imply "the necessity of . . . a radical revision of our attitude toward the problem of physical reality" (60). This revised picture of reality has much in common with the world depicted in *The Third Policeman*, and Charles Kemnitz has even argued that such modern scientific theories provide the structural principles upon which O'Brien's book is based:

It is the fully developed theory of quantum mechanics . . . that governs the narration in *The Third Policeman;* quantum mechanics is the atomic theory at work and doing untold destruction in the parish patrolled by Sergeant Pluck. (56)

Kemnitz's argument is tantalizing, though rather farfetched, and his attempts to make *The Third Policeman* sound like another version of George Gamow's *Mr. Tompkins in Wonderland* probably go too far.[13] However, numerous elements of O'Brien's novel are usefully illuminated through recourse to the theories of modern physics. These include Sergeant Pluck's "Atomic Theory," which argues that bicycle riders are in danger of exchanging atoms with their bicycles to the point that the riders themselves are more bicycle than human, while the bicycles are more human than machine.[14] And MacCruiskeen echoes a number of

13. Gamow was a physicist whose stories (later reprinted with additions as *Mr Tompkins in Paperback*) were written exclusively to illustrate scientific principles. O'Brien, by contrast, is a novelist whose fiction sometimes happens to resonate with certain concepts from science. For those interested in zeitgeist arguments, it is interesting to note that Gamow's collection of stories depicting bizarre worlds in which the rules of relativity and quantum physics apply on an everyday macro level were written at approximately the same time as *The Third Policeman*, in 1938 and 1939. Many people at this time were highly fascinated by the implications of the revolution in modern physics, though perhaps lacking an appreciation of some of the more ominous of those implications. O'Brien's *Dalkey Archive* resurrects many of the themes of *The Third Policeman*, but (having been written after World War II and the development of the atomic bomb) takes a noticeably more apocalyptic tone.

14. Kemnitz explicates this theory in terms of modern physics (65). Unfortunately

modern physical theories when he expounds on the existence of "omnium," a universal substance of which everything, both matter and energy, is made (109–11).[15] Finally, the dialogue between *The Third Policeman* and quantum physics is important from the point of view of the epistemology of futility depicted in the former. One of the best-known formulations of quantum physics is the Heisenberg Uncertainty Principle, which once and for all recognized a limit on the epistemological certainty available to scientists by suggesting that it is impossible *in principle* ever to know certain basic facts about nature beyond a certain point.

In particular, Heisenberg's Principle states that the product of any two noncommuting conjugate variables (examples include position and momentum, and energy and time) cannot be known beyond a specific amount of uncertainty—a principle that applies on all levels, but whose result is only significant in the realm of the very small, that is, the subatomic. To Heisenberg, this uncertainty arises because the direct measurement of reality is hopelessly compromised by the fact that the observer himself is a part of that reality and must interact with it in order to measure it. "[W]hat we observe is not nature in itself, but nature exposed to our method of questioning" (*Physics* 58). In other words he suggests, like Nietzsche, that our access to Truth is belated and indirect, caught in a loop of self-reference.[16]

Among the most striking manifestations of science in O'Brien's book are the various fantastic inventions of Policeman MacCruiskeen, which also participate in the motif of the infinite regression. MacCruiskeen shows the narrator a small chest, whose impeccable and elaborate workmanship is highly impressive. In fact, the chest is so exquisite that the only thing worthy of being stored in it is an identical chest of slightly smaller dimension. To the narrator's amazement, MacCruiskeen extracts

---

for his argument, it appears that O'Brien may have gotten the idea for this human-bicycle interaction from the way characters in *Tristram Shandy* interact with their "hobby-horses." See Clissmann (354n).

15. MacCruiskeen's conception of "omnium" partakes both of Einstein's work on the interchangeability of mass and energy and of the work of Niels Bohr and others on the dual wave/particle nature of matter and energy. It also has to do with the recognition that all matter is ultimately composed of certain fundamental subatomic particles that are themselves the same regardless of the nature of the matter they compose.

16. Bohr's more directly philosophical alternative explanation of the Uncertainty Principle sounds even more Nietzschean than does Heisenberg's. Bohr argues that the effect is fundamentally related to the nature of language, which inherently forces a distinction between subject and object, a distinction that does not accord with reality on the subatomic level. For a detailed treatment of Bohr's philosophy, see Hooker (132–209).

such a chest, and this sequence continues, with the policeman producing progressively smaller chests until reaching one "so small that it looked like a bug or a tiny piece of dirt except that there was a glitter from it" (73).

But this process can never come to an end, because each contained box must also be a container—there will never be a final box. At this point, MacCruiskeen (now having to use special equipment) begins to extract a still smaller box, which is invisible even with a magnifying glass. MacCruiskeen elaborates:

> "Six years ago they began to get invisible, glass or no glass. Nobody has ever seen the last five I made because no glass is strong enough to make them big enough to be regarded truly as the smallest things ever made."
> (74)

In short, the chests disappear into the realm beyond human perception, again calling into question the human ability ever to reach an epistemological bottom. This motif is made more explicit later when Michael Gilhaney accidentally knocks one of MacCruiskeen's invisible boxes off onto the floor, precipitating a frantic search. Gilhaney, realizing the pointlessness of searching for an imperceivable object (and doubting that the tiny chest even really exists), decides to humor MacCruiskeen by pretending to have found the chest and to put it back on the table. But this Emperor's-New-Clothes routine ends with a final twist—MacCruiskeen claims that Gilhaney *did* in fact find the chest and replace it on the table, only without knowing it! (114).[17]

The truth of MacCruiskeen's assertion here is, like all Truth, ultimately unknowable. This is a difficult fact for the narrator, with his epistemological inclinations, to accept. Indeed, he is made extremely uneasy by MacCruiskeen's invisible boxes in general, which infect him with a sudden vertiginous sense of terror. As the boxes approach the realm of the infinitely small, the narrator explains the effect:

17. Imperceivable objects are a specialty of MacCruiskeen's. He has a spear that appears to prick the narrator while still six inches away from him because its true point is so fine as to be invisible (67–68). And he plays a wondrous musical instrument that makes a sound that only he can hear (105). MacCruiskeen's marvelous inventions are what David Hayman has called "impossible objects." According to Hayman these "impossible objects" exploit the techniques of verisimilitude and rational discourse to undermine belief (52). In short, the technique calls into question the distinction between truth and fiction, a distinction that is obviously critical for epistemological investigation.

> At this point I became afraid. What he was doing was no longer won-
> derful but terrible. I shut my eyes and prayed that he would stop while
> still doing things that were at least possible for a man to do. (73)

The narrator here is showing a typical human discomfort when coming
face to face with the bottomlessness of infinity. Infinity is a concept that
eludes the attempts of human epistemology to reach final conclusions, so
much so that the archepistemologist Descartes considered the very fact
that we can even conceive of the infinite as proof of God's existence—
from where else could such a concept arise?

Jorge Luis Borges points out the conceptual power of infinity:

> There is a concept which corrupts and upsets all others. I refer not to
> Evil, whose limited realm is that of ethics; I refer to the infinite. (202)

Borges's concern with infinity extends especially into the phenomenon of
infinite regression as actuated by self-reference. His story "The Aleph"
shows this concern in a way that bears obvious similarities to much of
O'Brien's work. The story features a tiny box that contains the entire
universe, which then by definition must contain the tiny box, and so on.
Borges discusses this effect directly in his essay "Partial Magic in the
Quixote" (193–96). He notes that the same effect was described by Jo-
siah Royce in 1899 in discussing the example of a map that is traced in
the soil of England—a map so detailed that it includes itself, and so on
to infinity. Borges then relates this situation to the unsettling effects of
certain works of literature:

> Why does it disturb us that the map be included in the map and the
> thousand and one nights in the book of the *Thousand and One Nights*?
> Why does it disturb us that Don Quixote be a reader of the *Quixote* and
> Hamlet a spectator of *Hamlet*? I believe I have found the reason: these
> inversions suggest that if the characters of a fictional work can be
> readers or spectators, we, its readers and spectators, can be fictitious.
> (196)

Borges's comment seems particularly applicable to the nested narratives of *At Swim-Two-Birds*, but his understanding of the disturbing effects of such infinite regressions also usefully illuminates the discomfort
felt by the narrator of *The Third Policeman* when faced with Mac-
Cruiskeen's invisible boxes. For O'Brien's narrator such nesting effects
result in the loss of a stable ground for knowledge even of one's own
existence, leading to an understandable discomfort. Nietzsche himself
makes quite clear his belief that a true recognition of the infinitely self-

referential nature of all knowledge would not be tolerable to mankind, that it would lead to immediate insanity if comprehended directly. To cope with this problem, Nietzsche suggests that we rely on myth and on fictional models for reality—these are the means by which humanity can engage the chaos of reality and still remain sane. Nietzsche suggests that the "true constitution of things" may be so opposed to the presuppositions of life, that we must mask and fictionalize reality in order to live. According to Granier, "Nietzsche calls this masking *art*. Art is the veil of appearance thrown over the horrors of chaos" (138). Thus, "interpretation is synonymous with imposing sense, with molding chaos, with drawing a world of luminous figures out of what is hidden by the night of ignorance, impotence, and death" (Granier 140).

The potential damaging effect of looking directly into the abyss is dramatized directly in *The Third Policeman*. The mysterious Policeman Fox is apparently insane as a result of having peered inside one of Mac-Cruiskeen's fantastic boxes directly to perceive one of the ineffable colors therein. And as a grotesque band of one-legged "hoppy men" charge toward the station to free the narrator from captivity, MacCruiskeen proposes to fend them off by painting his bicycle this abysmal color and then riding it in view of the attackers, driving them insane (165).

The implication is that, not only are some questions unanswerable, but perhaps it is dangerous even to pursue certain answers. This suggestion has obvious religious resonances; Anne Clissmann interprets the skepticism toward human systems of knowledge shown by O'Brien in *The Third Policeman* and *The Dalkey Archive* as an indication of O'Brien's belief that, after a point, we should eschew human understanding and simply place our trust in God. For Christianity, after all, there are limits to the knowledge that humans are supposed to acquire, and it is worth recalling that the Original Sin of humanity consisted in going beyond a prescribe epistemological limit.[18] To Clissmann, then, O'Brien in *The Third Policeman* and *The Dalkey Archive* "emerges as a deeply religious man, trusting that the questions which are unanswerable will one day be answered completely" (323).

Clissmann's opinion about O'Brien's own personal belief may be entirely accurate. However, inadvertently or not, O'Brien has created a textual climate in these books in which any escape from the infinite regression of the epistemology of futility through an appeal to God is

18. Indeed, Hunt relates *The Third Policeman* to the myth of the Fall, suggesting that the narrator is a sort of Everyman figure who "must also bear the burden of the Fall. In this respect Mathers 'black box' is recognizable as that burden and as death which is a consequence of seeking forbidden knowledge" (65).

strongly called into question. The infinite perspective to which O'Brien's various regressions lead can be interpreted either as an argument that there must be a God (because only God can be infinite) or as an argument that the very concept of God as a stopping place for such regressions makes no sense. When the narrator of *The Third Policeman* undergoes his vertiginous vision concerning the infinite nesting of bodies within bodies, the implication is that the process moves in the other direction as well—perhaps "God" is merely the sub-God of some greater God, and so on. In fact, O'Brien suggests that the limitations of human knowledge are such that we would not know God if we saw him, arguing that it is impossible from our human point of view to distinguish between God and the Devil. Thus, the De Selby of *The Dalkey Archive* (a somewhat revised reinscription of the de Selby of *The Third Policeman*) suggests that, because the victors write the histories of wars, we cannot be certain that the biblical account of Lucifer's rebellion is accurate. "For if—I repeat *if*—the decision had gone the other way and God had been vanquished, who but Lucifer would be certain to put about the other and opposite story?" (22–23).

The absence of a theological anchor in *The Third Policeman* can of course be partially attributed to the fact that most of the action occurs in a sort of hell, the one place where one would not expect to find God anyway.[19] But religion is traditionally the kind of discourse in which one seeks precisely the kind of ultimate Truth that *The Third Policeman* seems designed to mock. Indeed, Roy Hunt finds religion itself to be one of the principal objects of the book's satire. For Hunt, the book shows that

> confronted by the unsettling truth of the unattainability of truth, people seek comfort and security in systems where truth is indubitable. Naturally enough O'Brien examines the systems in which people have traditionally placed their most trust: science and religion. Both, finally, are shown to be unsatisfactory refuges. (68)[20]

It is, in fact, the engagement with specific discourses of authority like science, religion, and philosophy that gives *The Third Policeman* the better part of its critical energy—though at all times it should be kept in

19. The epistemological confusion of the text can be partially attributed to the hellish setting as well. One might compare this setting with the hell of Dante's *Inferno*, which is heavily informed by interpretive confusion, a confusion that gradually clears as the pilgrim Dante mounts toward heaven.

20. Bakhtin notes that carnivalesque representations of hell are particularly subversive of religious (especially Catholic) authority, as that authority places such emphasis on hell as an area of "gloom, fear, and intimidation" (*Rabelais* 395).

mind that the inherent ambiguity of O'Brien's own text warns against the establishment of literature as a replacement discourse of authority. Such discourses seek the kind of absolute answers of which O'Brien is skeptical everywhere in his work. In *At Swim-Two-Birds* the Good Fairy explains this position during the epistemological proceedings of the trial of Dermot Trellis:

> Answers do not matter so much as questions, said the Good Fairy. A good question is very hard to answer. The better the question the harder the answer. There is no answer at all to a very good question. (291)

And as Sergeant Pluck tells the narrator in *The Third Policeman*, "The first beginnings of wisdom is to ask questions but never to answer any" (59).

This emphasis on questions as opposed to answers again undercuts epistemological inquiry and anticipates the mode of discourse referred to by Richard Rorty as hermeneutics. To Rorty, Western philosophy since Descartes (and to some extent since Plato) has been dominated by an epistemological search for ultimate knowledge of Truth, where Truth is defined as an accurate representation of the way things "really" are in a fundamental sense. Thus, with the epistemological view:

> The notion of knowledge as accurate representation lends itself naturally to the notion that certain sorts of representations, certain expressions, certain processes are "basic," "privileged," and "foundational." (*Philosophy* 318–19)

The Western epistemological tradition results in an addiction to knowledge, and it is this addiction that Rorty attacks. The epistemological drive to know also results in a loss of freedom and a limiting of possibilities, encouraging the development of privileged and hegemonic discourses. What Rorty calls the hermeneutic approach, on the other hand, requires that no one discourse be privileged above all others because this privileging ultimately leads to the impoverishing notion that all discourses should model themselves on the privileged discourse. Thus in hermeneutics, variety of discourse is encouraged in order to allow for richer development of ideas and to keep the "conversation" moving:

> Hermeneutics sees the relations between various discourses as those of strands in a possible conversation, a conversation which presupposes no disciplinary matrix which unites the speakers, but where the hope of

> agreement is never lost so long as the conversation lasts. . . . For her-
> meneutics, to be rational is to be willing to refrain from epistemology—
> from thinking that there is a special set of terms in which all contribu-
> tions to the conversation should be put—and to be willing to pick up
> the jargon of the interlocutor rather than translating it into one's own.
> (*Philosophy* 318)

Nietzsche is one of the "edifying" philosophers identified by Rorty as pursuing a project that is consistent with what he terms hermeneutics. And the comparison with Nietzsche (and with Rorty's reading of Nietzsche) helps to illustrate that the demystification of epistemology set forth in works like *The Third Policeman* does not necessarily lead to nega-tivism or nihilism, but simply to pragmatism. Rorty cites Nietzsche, along with William James, as the great forerunners of his modern prag-matic philosophy:

> This was the step taken by Nietzsche and William James. Their contri-
> bution was to replace romanticism by pragmatism. Instead of saying
> that the discovery of vocabularies could bring hidden secrets to light,
> they said that new ways of speaking could help get us what we want.
> (*Consequences* 150)

The pragmatic nature of Nietzsche's project is emphasized by Breazeale in his discussion of Nietzsche's notion of truth. Nietzsche does not reject the idea of truth entirely. Rather, he simply makes truth an object of pragmatic interpretation because of the infinitely self-referential nature of human knowledge. Thus, Breazeale notes that, while Nietzsche does deny the existence of ultimate, transcendental truths, he does not deny the fact that some interpretations of reality are more valuable to us than others. "Understood in this second sense, knowing is not an at-tempt to mirror an independently real world, but rather a process of accommodating ourselves to the world in which we live and that world to us: truths are humanly constructed instruments designed to serve hu-man purposes" (xxxii). Breazeale's view not only highlights the fact that some metaphorically created "truths" are better than others but also shows the importance of such truths to humanity's basic well being. Time and again, in fact, Nietzsche himself launches furious attacks on nihilism. It is his contention that beliefs are vital, even if they are beliefs in fiction. Thus, he writes that the "falsest judgments . . . are the most indispensible ones for us . . . without a constant falsification of the world . . . man could not live" (*Beyond* 202, pt. 1. sec. 4) and that "a belief can be a condition of life and nonetheless be false" (*Will* 268, sec. 483).

As Rorty has recently argued with such energy, the value of a concept lies not in its ultimate "truth" or "falsity," but in its usefulness to (as Wallace Stevens said of poetry) "help men to live their lives" (29). In fact, Nietzsche's work suggests that the traditional distinction between truth and fiction no longer exists:

> What then is truth? A movable host of metaphors, metonymies, and anthropomorphisms: in short, a sum of human relations which have been poetically and rhetorically intensified, transferred, and embellished, and which, after long usage, seem to a people to be fixed, canonical, and binding. Truths are illusions which we have forgotten are illusions; they are metaphors that have become worn out and have been drained of sensuous force, coins that have lost their embossing and are now considered as metal and no longer as coins. ("On Truth" 84; sec. 1)

This hardening of illusion into "truth" is always for Nietzsche insidious, and indicates the necessity for perpetual and continual re-creation (coining?) of fresh metaphors.[21] Fictions must be capable of being discarded when they outlive their usefulness.

Such interrogations of the boundaries between truth and fiction form a central part of O'Brien's project. And the emphasis on creation in Nietzsche illuminates the way a radical skepticism toward epistemology can lead, not to impoverishment, but to richness. The defamiliarizing strangeness of works like *The Third Policeman* enriches our conceptions of the world by suggesting alternative conceptions of reality that escape the limiting confines of traditional systems of knowledge. As Hillis Miller has aptly observed, one of the principal features linking various disciplines in the twentieth century is a growing appreciation of the fact that the world is nothing if not strange:

> Twentieth-century thought—in linguistics, in psychology, in biology, in ethnology and sociology, in atomic physics, and in astrophysics—has been characterized by this recognition that the realms of man and nature are stranger than we had thought, along with the unceasing attempt to find out the laws of this strangeness and so make the unfamiliar familiar. (18–19)

---

21. The emphasis on flux in Nietzsche can also be illuminated in terms of his denial of cause and effect. In a strictly causal Newtonian universe, there is also change, but any future change can in principle be predicted from the state of the universe at any given time. Quantum theory, of course, denies that such predictions can be made. Nietzsche's conception of change is clearly of the quantum, rather than the Newtonian, type.

But, *The Third Policeman* tells us, this unceasing attempt is doomed to failure because the world is infinitely stranger and more complex than our systems of description are capable of comprehending. As O'Toole points out, much of the vertiginous effect of the book arises from the way O'Brien employs such a complex mixture of different scientific and philosophical theories in constructing the complex and incomprehensible world of his text (216). This dense conceptual stew serves as a commentary on the general twentieth-century crisis in authority, on the modern lack of faith in any one approach to knowledge. Both modern physics and the philosophy of Nietzsche participate in this crisis in important ways; thus, it is entirely apt that they function so well as glosses for O'Brien's own text. This crisis can be terrifying and unsettling, like the world of O'Brien's text, and one might certainly read in *The Third Policeman* a nostalgic yearning for a return to the security of well-established authority. But *The Third Policeman* shows the typical doubleness of O'Brien's writing, and so it can also be read to suggest the invidiousness of authoritative approaches in general. Perhaps modern life is made difficult less by the lack of authority than by our continuing (and futile) quest for ultimate authority. O'Brien's text shows that the Enlightenment project of gaining a complete understanding and domination of nature through the resources of human reason is a futile one. *The Third Policeman* reflects many of the concepts and concerns of modern physics and philosophy, though its main force may be to parody the attempts of such human endeavors to grasp a reality that is ultimately unknowable. In this sense, O'Brien's project in the book parallels those of modern thinkers like Nietzsche and Rorty, who have similarly challenged traditional methods of seeking the Truth. It should be remembered, however, that *The Third Policeman*, like all of O'Brien's work, contains a great deal of self-parody as well.[22] O'Brien thus avoids setting up his own work as a substitute for the authorities undermined in his book. As Lanters points out, *The Third Policeman* resembles *At Swim-Two-Birds* in that one of the important targets of its satire involves the machinations of would-be "tyrannical" authors:

> O'Brien's belief that man never learns from experience and never attains self-knowledge leads him to the inevitable conclusion that it is a sign of

22. In this vein it is also useful to remember that there is a great deal of comedy in the book, and its tone is by no means unequivocally dark. The book has thus drawn contrasting responses from critics. Silverthorne, for example, finds that the book is informed by an unrelieved tone of pessimism upon which O'Brien builds "an impregnable superstructure of frustration" (83). But Jerry McGuire finds that the book does offer hopeful alternatives that allow the reader to see beyond the text itself and "save the reader . . . from being entirely absorbed, destroyed" by the text's own atmosphere of futility (121).

foolishness and conceit in a writer to make bold statements about the world and to create the impression, through excess of imagination, that he understands more than he does. (281)

Just as the book mocks the pretensions of scientists, philosophers, and theologians to be able to know the Truth, it also suggests that the authors of fictional texts don't have all the answers, either. As a result, critics of the epistemological tradition like Nietzsche and Rorty, as well as fiction writers like O'Brien himself are also partially implicated in the book's parody. For O'Brien there are more things in heaven and earth than are dreamt of in our philosophy or science but also in our literature.

5

Linguistic Oppression and Cultural Definition in Ireland

The Poor Mouth and the Mother Tongue

In *The Poor Mouth* O'Brien shifts his sights to the West of Ireland, depicting life among the rural peasants of the Gaeltacht. He shows the hardship and squalor of Gaeltacht life with a critical and biting wit reminiscent of the satire of Swift in works like "A Modest Proposal." O'Brien's satire gains a special force from his effective creation of a dialogic opposition between the reality of peasant life and certain romanticized and condescending fantasies about that life that are promulgated by more "sophisticated" outsiders, including the more urban Irish. *The Poor Mouth* thus once again places O'Brien squarely in the tradition of Menippean satire. But this book differs from O'Brien's other major works—and from the works of Irish writers like Swift, Joyce, and Beckett—in a very important way. It was written (as *An Béal Bocht*) in Gaelic, and this central fact opens up numerous unique possibilities for commentary on life in Ireland. *The Poor Mouth* will never gain the literary status of Dante's *Commedia* or Chaucer's *Canterbury Tales* (and does not deserve to do so), but O'Brien's decision to write the book in Gaelic carries many of the same cultural implications as Dante's decision to write in his vernacular Tuscan Italian or Chaucer's choice of Middle English for his poetry. And O'Brien's choice is even more significant amidst a twentieth century in which one of the most prominent and distinctive intellectual trends has involved the growing recognition of the central importance of language to the way we conceive of, indeed construct, our reality.

In a recent defense of his controversial *The Satanic Verses*, Salman

Rushdie declares that central to the purposes of the book is "the process of reclaiming language from one's opponents" ("Good" 54). This comment, coming from a writer with Rushdie's complex Indian-British cultural background, obviously resonates with much of the recent critical interest in language as an aspect of colonization (and of decolonization). Rushdie's reclamation metaphor particularly points toward a potential application of Bakhtin's theories of parody and of dialogism to this debate. And elsewhere Rushdie shows a highly Bakhtinian appreciation for the historicity and political embeddedness of language, arguing that the vestiges of empire are still to be found in the "cadences" of the English language itself. On the other hand, he sees the political charge that inheres in language to be potentially energizing. He argues that much "vitality and excitement" can be derived from attempts to "decolonize" the language, citing a number of contemporary writers like Chinua Achebe and Ngugi wa Thiong'o who are resisting the history of imperialism that inheres within the language by "busily forging English into new shapes":

> But of course a good deal more than formal, stylistic alteration is going on in this new fiction. And perhaps above all, what is going on is politics. . . . There are very few major writers in the new English literatures who do not place politics at the very centre of their art. ("Empire" 8)

In this same article, Rushdie cites the great Irish writers Joyce, Beckett, and O'Brien as predecessors, and the identification of Ireland with this important effort seems particularly appropriate. Irish writers, forced in the main to write in the language of an occupying imperial power, have nevertheless been able to reach a staggering level of literary achievement in this century. Yet, despite the prominence of Irish writers in modern "British" literature, many of the leading Irish authors have shown a certain discomfort with the English language that they have inherited from their imperial oppressors. Perhaps the paradigmatic moment of this phenomenon occurs in the famous passage in Joyce's *Portrait of the Artist as a Young Man* in which Stephen Dedalus suddenly becomes intensely aware of the political orientation of language, comparing his own speech to that of the English dean of studies at his school:

> The language in which we are speaking is his before it is mine. How different are the words *home, Christ, ale, master,* on his lips and on mine! I cannot speak or write these words without unrest of spirit. His language, so familiar and so foreign, will always be for me an acquired speech. (189, Joyce's emphases)

The resultant sense of secondariness, of isolation from the language one has been taught to use, is expressed even more strongly by Beckett, from Watt's perceived incommensurability between a pot and the word "pot" to Molloy's "nameless things" and "thingless names" to the total linguistic alienation of The Unnamable:

> It's of me now I must speak, even if I have to do it with their language, it will be a start, a step towards silence and the end of madness, the madness of having to speak and not being able to, except of things that don't concern me, that don't count, that I don't believe, that they have crammed me full of to prevent me from saying who I am . . . I have no language but theirs. (325, my ellipsis)

Although in Beckett there is a sense of alienation from *all* language, one should not discount the political resonances that inevitably arise from any discussion of the foreignness of language in a writer who grew up under conditions of linguistic colonialism. Numerous reasons have been given (by Beckett and others) for Beckett's eventual turn to French as his primary language of expression, but a desire to escape from the shadows of English imperial domination must surely figure prominently among these.

Similarly, Joyce reacted to the colonial echoes inherent in English by employing an increasingly polyglot means of expression that eventually led him to the complex heteroglossic goulash of *Finnegans Wake*.[1] Both Beckett and Joyce displayed considerable facility with multiple languages, though neither of them confronted English linguistic domination through the most obvious means—learning and using their native Gaelic. Beckett hardly mentions Gaelic in his work, except for passing sardonic comments like Molloy's expression of his total inability to interpret tears and laughter: "they are so much Gaelic to me" (37). Joyce confronts the issue more explicitly, as in the encounters of young Stephen with Gaelic Leaguers in *Portrait* and especially in *Stephen Hero*. And there are certainly numerous Gaelic echoes in Joyce's attempt to reclaim English for his own use. But Stephen's eventual rejection of Gaelic as a vehicle of obscurantism and superstition seems to be one of the rare times when his views were substantially in accord with Joyce's own.[2]

1. The seeds of Wakean language seem to have been planted quite early in Joyce's career. Thus in his apprentice work *Stephen Hero*, he has Cranly speak in a language "the base of which was Latin and the superstructure of which was composed of Irish, French and German" (106).

2. In *Stephen Hero* Stephen argues that the Irish Nationalists "encourage the study of

Of the three leading modern Irish fiction writers, then, it was left for O'Brien to explore directly the potential of Gaelic as an alternative means of literary expression. Not coincidentally, O'Brien was the only one of these three writers who remained in Ireland throughout his career, and for many years he wrote newspaper columns (under his Gaelic *nom de plume* Myles na gCopaleen) that alternated between English and Gaelic.[3] And in *An Béal Bocht* he wrote a major work in Gaelic. Ironically, the translation *The Poor Mouth* has had far more readers than the original *An Béal Bocht* (as so few readers know Gaelic), and this displacement of the Gaelic original by its English translation becomes an interesting story of English imperial domination in its own right. In addition, the inability of most readers to understand O'Brien's book in the original becomes one of his more striking statements on the difficulty of communication within the linguistic context of modern Ireland. Having no Gaelic I work here of necessity with *The Poor Mouth*, while trying to remain aware of such implications.[4]

The Poor Mouth was not only originally written in Gaelic, but it is largely *about* Gaelic, and about the place of Gaelic in Irish culture. In this sense the book participates centrally in the tradition of Bakhtin's "Second Line" novel, which is informed by Menippean energies and in which "language in the novel not only represents, but itself serves as the object of representation" (*Dialogic* 49). *The Poor Mouth* is highly dialogic and quite rhetorically complex, with much of its satire apparently being directed not at the English linguistic domination of Ireland, but at what O'Brien saw as the excesses of modern writers (and translators) of Gaelic. This satire is partially effected through parody of specific Irish writers like Tomás O Criomhthain and Séamas O Grianna, though much of the force of this parody is necessarily lost in the English translation.[5] More-

---

Irish that their flocks may be more safely protected from the «wolves of disbelief»; they consider it as an opportunity to withdraw the people into a past of literal, implicit faith" (54).

3. It is true, however, that the columns tended more and more toward English as his career progressed—ostensibly because more readers were available who could understand English.

4. Critics have tended to feel a little uneasy about this same necessity. For example, Sue Asbee begins her chapter on *The Poor Mouth* with an apology for being so presumptuous as to discuss the book in English translation (71). Asbee goes on to elaborate, noting O'Brien's distaste for English translations of Gaelic works like Tomás O Criomhthain's *An tOileánach (The Islandman)* (71–74). O'Brien himself resisted the translation of *An Béal Bocht* because he felt that English simply could not convey many of the linguistic nuances that were so important to the book. It thus did not appear until after his death.

5. Indeed, though *The Poor Mouth* carries resonances of a long-lost Irish past, it par-

over, this parody can itself be quite complex, as O'Brien greatly admired some of his Gaelic models (especially O Criomhthain) and clearly did not intend to mock them.[6] Instead, O'Brien's parody is of the sort described by Bakhtin as "an intentional dialogized hybrid. Within it, languages and styles actively and mutually illuminate one another" (*Dialogic* 76). In addition, there is much direct satirical commentary on the Gaelic language itself (and on certain academics who have turned it into an object of study). However, one should again be cautious in interpreting this satire. *The Poor Mouth* is not an attack on Gaelic or on the Gaels. If anything, it is a sort of paean to the language and a plea that the people be seen in their concrete reality and not as mere stereotypes.

In one representative episode of the book a "gentleman from Dublin" travels through the countryside of O'Brien's Corkadoragha recording examples of authentic spoken Gaelic in order to study it and to save it for posterity. He meets with much opposition from the superstitious peasants, though he does make some headway by bribing them with alcohol. And at last he manages, under cover of darkness, to record an example of Gaelic so excellent that his academic fortune is made. Admittedly, none of the experts for whom he plays his recording can make out a word of it, but that is all for the better. After all, the gentleman knows that "good Gaelic is difficult but that the best Gaelic of all is well-nigh unintelligible" (44). But this Gaelic is particularly unintelligible—especially because what the gentleman unknowingly recorded was in fact the grunting of an unruly pig.[7]

This episode thus comments both upon the obscurity of Gaelic as a language and upon the incompetence of the condescending urban academicians who study it. Moreover, this humorous little episode carries some highly serious political suggestions. The dominant (English-speaking) elements of Irish society are the ones in command of the various

---

ticipates in a very contemporary development, the rise in popularity of Gaelic autobiographies in Ireland. On this phenomenon, for which O Criomhthain was an important inspiration, see McNab.

6. Monique Gallagher presents an extended comparison of *The Poor Mouth* and *The Islandman*, noting that "when O'Brien parodied or ironically transcribed passages from *The Islandman*, he did not for a moment stop admiring his model" (240).

7. This academic takes his tapes to Berlin in order to achieve recognition. Granted Germany was long a traditional center for Gaelic studies. But there may also be political undertones in this gesture toward Berlin. *An Béal Bocht* first appeared in 1941, during the height of Hitler's power in Germany. The implied link between the racist policies of Nazi Germany and the treatment of the Gaels in Ireland greatly strengthens the political impact of this episode. Note that the German experts also believe the recorded "Gaelic" to be authentic.

languages of power; they are the ones in charge of definition and classification. As such, they regard the Gaels, and their language, as inferior. So much so that, to certain elements of the society, Gaels are indistinguishable from pigs.

Bakhtin's now-famous reading of Rabelais emphasizes that dominant social groups tend to create hierarchical distinctions through which they can establish and confirm their superiority over marginal groups. In particular, marginal groups tend to be associated with images of filth and decay (like excrement and death) that the dominant groups wish to regard as Other than themselves.[8] Bakhtin's important conceptualization of the carnival explores the ways in which carnivalesque energies act to overturn such artificial hierarchies. Similarly, the central Bakhtinian notion of dialogism calls into question any neat hierarchical separation between groups by showing an inextricable mutual involvement between different social groups in terms of the use of language. *The Poor Mouth*, with its frequent carnivalesque humor and its central emphasis on the social implications of linguistic differences in Ireland, provides an ideal venue for the exploration of Bakhtin's two key concepts of carnival and dialogism within the context of O'Brien's work.

For Bakhtin a principal source of dialogue in the novel arises from the relationship between an author and his narrator, the inherent difference in these positions generating dialogic energy in even the most ostensibly monologic text. In some texts, this effect is enhanced through the use of a narrator who differs from the author in particularly obvious or significant ways. For example, the Russian tradition of *skaz* narration typically employs techniques like intentional solecisms, provincial dialects, and oral syntax to separate its narrators from their more literate authors. The *skaz* technique has its roots in the tradition of Russian folk tales and has been prominently used by modern Russian writers like Zamyatin and Zoshchenko. The technique was prominently discussed by the Russian Formalists (especially Eichenbaum), and in *The Dialogic Imagination* Bakhtin identifies *skaz* as one of the most effective ways in which a novel can import folk energies and "extraliterary" materials, adding to the richness of voices in the text. The *skaz* distance between narrator and author is most commonly established through the use of a narrator who is uneducated, even illiterate, and whose style of narration thus has a down-to-earth, oral quality clearly distinct from what one

8. These images can be roughly associated with what Julia Kristeva has termed the "abject." On this motif of association of marginal groups with images of filth and degradation, also see Stallybrass and White.

might expect from a sophisticated author.[9] This technique is, of course, very much that employed in *The Poor Mouth*, whose Irish peasant narrator differs quite markedly from the urban, educated O'Brien, creating dialogic and ironic effects that importantly enrich the novel. Most obviously, the narrator is undermined by his own obvious ignorance, frequently seeming to make points very different from the ones he seeks. But this difference cuts both ways, also serving as a reminder that literary figurations of the Irish peasantry are often produced by urban observers who are in no position truly to understand life in the Irish countryside.

The dialogic texture of *The Poor Mouth* is also greatly enriched by its inherent dialogue between English and Gaelic. O'Brien is writing the book after two decades of "independence" from Britain in the Irish Free State, but his book makes it quite clear that vestiges of British domination remain, and that certain social, economic, and (particularly) linguistic hierarchies put in place during the centuries of British rule are still very real factors in Irish life.[10] These hierarchies are particularly dramatized in O'Brien's book by the radical alterity that exists between the relatively sophisticated English-speaking Irishmen of Dublin and the poor Gaelic-speaking peasants of Corkadoragha.

That speakers of English are in total control of the official mechanisms of power in Ireland is dramatized by two specific episodes in *The Poor Mouth*. In the first of these we accompany narrator Bonaparte O'Coonassa, during his first day at school. School, of course, is taught in English, and when the master asks the boy's name, the boy cannot understand because he knows only Gaelic. Finally, one of his classmates interprets the question for him, and the boy begins to respond by citing his full name (and pedigree) in Gaelic. The master angrily cracks him over the skull and screams at him: "Yer nam, said he, is Jams O'Donnell!" (30).

One after another, the narrator's classmates repeat this experience of linguistic humiliation and its corporal reinforcement. Afterwards the boy expresses to his mother his amazement that every boy in the school turns out to be named "Jams O'Donnell." She responds with resignation:

> If that's the way, said she, don't you understand that it's Gaels that live in this side of the country and that they can't escape from fate? It was always said and written that every Gaelic youngster is hit on his first school day because he doesn't understand English and the foreign form

9. See Titunik for an excellent discussion of the *skaz* technique.
10. While Gaelic is actually the official language of the Republic of Ireland, most people there still speak English, and Gaelic appears to be dying out.

of his name and that no one has any respect for him because he's Gaelic to the marrow. (33–34)

The Gaels, in short, are introduced to oppression and adversity (especially of a linguistic kind) quite early on. The suggestion that, to outsiders, all Gaels are named "Jams O'Donnell" indicates the way the Gaels are treated not as individual human beings, but as faceless and interchangeable members of an excluded and inferior group. Naming would seem to be the simplest and most straightforward application of language, but in *The Poor Mouth* the sliding signification indicated elsewhere in O'Brien extends even to names, with the same name sliding freely among all the male Gaels. But if all the Gaels have the same name, then in a sense they have no name at all; and the various Jams O'Donnells of *The Poor Mouth* are thus in very much the same alienated condition as the nameless narrator of *The Third Policeman*.

Jacques Lacan has noted that naming is the paradigmatic example of linguistic tyranny. Just as this schoolmaster has selected "Jams O'Donnell" as the English label his students will bear even before they can speak English, so too are we all generally named before we can speak, labeled in language before we can choose our own labels. As Lacan points out,

> the subject, too, if he can appear to be the slave of language is all the more so of a discourse in the universal movement in which his place is already inscribed at birth, if only by virtue of his proper name. (*Écrits* 148).

Lacan's general formulation of the subject as a "slave of language" takes on a special political resonance when that language is imposed from without by an occupying foreign power. The schoolmaster's ability not only to name all of his students as "Jams O'Donnell," but to have them accept those names as proper, would appear to represent an example of total linguistic domination.[11]

The linguistic disadvantage of the Gaels in dealing with the official institutions of Irish society is further emphasized at the book's end. The narrator's father has been absent during his entire life, and at the end we learn that he has been absent because he was in prison. But the Gaels of *The Poor Mouth* are caught in an endless cycle of repetition, and the narrator in fact meets his father—or at least a man whom he takes for his

11. "Flann O'Brien" is itself but the best known of many pen names adopted by Brian O'Nolan. O'Nolan's tendency to adopt different names of his own choosing in different situations might be read as a form of resistance to this tyranny of naming.

father—for the first time at a train station as the latter returns from
prison while the former is being taken to prison for a crime he did not
commit. This cycle of imprisonment occurs largely because of the linguistic inability of the Gaels to deal with the legal system. The narrator describes his interrogation and trial:

> I have a faint memory of being in a noble palace; being a while with a
> great crowd of peelers who spoke to me and to one another in English;
> being yet another while in prison. I never understood a single item of
> all that happened around me nor one word of the conversation nor my
> interrogation. (122)

In the narrator's encounters with the educational and legal systems of
Ireland, the oppression suffered by the marginal, excluded Gaels seems
quite clear. However, O'Brien's treatment of the overall position of the
Gaels in Ireland is quite complex, and there are indications that the Gaels
themselves bear much of the responsibility for their predicament. As the
narrator's mother indicates in the passage cited above, the Gaels seem to
have accepted misfortune as the unavoidable fate of their race, to have
romanticized suffering itself into a central cultural myth. O'Brien's parody of the mythologization of suffering in Ireland resonates with a similar motif that occurs frequently in the work of Joyce, who depicts
numerous ways in which the glorification of suffering and sacrifice by
both the Catholic Church and by the Irish nationalists leads to a mode of
passive acceptance that makes the Irish particularly susceptible to domination by outside forces like the Church of Rome or the imperial forces
of Britain. A similar motif runs through almost all of O'Brien's work as
well, as in the tribulations undergone by Sweeny and Trellis in *At Swim-
Two-Birds* or the general miseries of the Irish peasants in *The Poor Mouth*,
and it is worth keeping in mind that there is a consistent element of
social satire in the strain of cruelty and violence that runs through
O'Brien's work.

In the case of *The Poor Mouth* it is important that the myths of suffering accepted by the Gaels arise not from indigenous sources, but are
imposed on them from without. One of the central difficulties of life in
O'Brien's Gaeltacht concerns the way the inhabitants tend to accept and
to enact the expectations created for them by the narratives of Gaelic life
brought to them by city dwellers. In addition, the Gaels themselves seem
to accept the innate superiority of English to Gaelic as a practical mode
of expression. In one episode, English linguistic imperialism comes directly to Corkadoragha, but it is greeted with surprising good humor by

the poor Gaelic inhabitants. The "Old-Grey-Fellow," O'Brien's arch-Gael, regards the event as an absolute windfall:

> Upon me soul, said he, I hear that the English Government is going to do great work for the good of the paupers here in this place, safe and saved may everyone be in this house! It is fixed to pay the likes of us two pounds a skull for every child of ours that speaks English instead of this thieving Gaelic. Trying to separate us from the Gaelic they are, praise be to them sempiternally! (35)[12]

Clearly, the Old-Fellow is cheered by the thought of those English pounds, though he is also excited by the prospects of escaping from Gaelic itself, a language which he sees as contributing to the unfortunate state of local life. He goes on to explain that "I don't think there'll be good conditions for the Gaels while . . . telling stories at night about the hardships and hard times of the Gaels in sweet words of Gaelic is natural to them" (35).

Unfortunately, the magnitude of the lucre associated with this project is limited for the Old-Fellow by the fact that there is only one child in his household—his grandson, the book's narrator. But there are rumors that the inspector who is taking the census of English-speaking children is "an aged crippled man without good sight and that he lacked enthusiasm for his work as well" (35). And so the resourceful Old-Fellow concocts a plan to increase his bounty from the English payout. Because his family (in typical Gaelic squalor) already shares its home with a large number of pigs, it only seems natural to dress these pigs as children in an attempt to increase the head count to a dozen or so. After all, "youngsters and piglets have the same habits and take notice that there's a close likeness between their skins" (36).

When the inspector arrives he elects not to come inside the house because the smell is too strong. And so he simply asks how many children in the household speak English, and the Old-Fellow replies: "Twalf, sor!" (37), with the pigs milling in the background to provide verification. To test the linguistic facility of these youngsters, the inspector simply asks the first one who presents himself (the narrator, of course) to reveal his name. "Jams O'Donnell, sor!" replies the boy enthusiastically.

12. The reference to the "English government" here might seem to place this episode in the years before Irish independence. However, in most cases in *The Poor Mouth,* the speakers of English who impinge upon the Gaels are Irish, not English. But nothing ever seems to change for the inhabitants of Corkadoragha, and it would appear irrelevant to their lives whether the political power that dominates them arises from London or from Dublin.

Satisfied, the inspector goes away to escape the stench, and a few days later the Old-Fellow receives his payment by mail.

This little vignette seems amusing enough, but, just as the careless inspector misses much of significance in this encounter, so too is there much here that could be missed without close and careful attention on the part of the reader. For example, the boy's reference to himself as "Jams O'Donnell" seems to imply his acceptance of the name given him at the English-speaking school, just as the Old-Fellow's willing acknowledgment of the similarity between pigs and Gaelic children seems to indicate a total capitulation to the kinds of cultural stereotypes that would make such associations. Yet, the victory for English linguistic imperialism is clearly incomplete because both the narrator and the Old-Fellow take these positions in order to subvert the project of the language inspector.

Bakhtin's comments on the dialogic nature of all discourse imply that no single group or attitude can ever dominate language entirely. In every society there will be a dominant discourse (actually, a family of discourses), but that discourse can only define itself in relation to other repressed discourses with which it maintains a dialogic tension. Thus, the very nature of language itself indicates that there will always be a possibility that opposing voices can arise, even if they must do so through parodic manipulation of the language of authority. For Bakhtin even the most dominant of discourses inherently contains the seeds of opposition and potential liberation.

In the case of O'Brien's narrator in *The Poor Mouth*, the opportunity for a parodic subversion of the movement by which he is named "Jams O'Donnell" in the school occurs quite quickly, and he reclaims this name for his own by using it against the census taker, thereby convincing this inspector that he speaks English. Moreover, because members of the inspector's social class seem firmly convinced that one Gael is as good as another, this small demonstration of linguistic facility is taken as representative of the whole family, serving as proof that the family pigs speak English as well. The narrator thus turns the tables on the oppressors and uses their smug confidence in their own superiority against them.

The narrator's reference to himself using this imposed name is thus truly double-voiced. To the inspector, it serves as a signal that the boy has been properly indoctrinated concerning his place in the linguistic order. But it also serves as a highly subversive indication that the speakers of English are not so superior as they would like to believe. Indeed, because the Gaels who are forced to learn English are to some extent bilingual, they have certain inherent linguistic advantages over their monolingual colonizers.[13] These advantages are made quite explicit in this same episode in the ostensibly polite references of both the narrator and the Old-Fellow to the census taker as "sor." He, of course, takes this as a sign of respect, with the inferior ability of the Gaels to speak English properly accounting for the inadvertent transformation of "sir" into "sor." Indeed, there is a Gaelic accent at work in this word, but not the kind the inspector thinks. "Sor" is a Gaelic word meaning "louse," so that once again the Gaels manage a dexterously double-voiced use of language that rings of submissiveness to the ear of the oppressor but that is in fact highly subversive.[14]

This entire episode would seem to represent a virtuoso performance in the use of an apparent acceptance of cultural stereotypes of the Gaels against the imposers of those stereotypes—a sort of cultural/linguistic jujitsu in which the strength of the oppressors is used against them. In this respect the use of pigs as surrogate children is particularly appropriate because pigs have historically occupied a special place in the dynamic by which dominant groups seek to identify marginal groups with images of filth and animality.[15] Moreover, in a variety of modern societies the epithet "pig" is commonly used to refer to those who display transgressive behavior, especially behavior that suggests the kind of filth from which polite society seeks to distance itself.

There seems to be a particularly strong association between pigs and degradation in the work of modern Irish writers. One thinks here of Leopold Bloom's transformation into a pig during his mortification in the "Circe" episode of *Ulysses*. And Pozzo in Beckett's *Waiting for Godot* constantly seeks to subjugate and humiliate his slave Lucky by calling him "pig." Vivian Mercier notes the significance of Pozzo's treatment of Lucky in terms of Irish social structures, pointing to the

> searing caricature of exploitation by one class or race of another that is represented in the Pozzo-Lucky relationship. . . . Pozzo's insistence on the goodness of his own heart and the dog-like devotion to him of

13. Importantly, though, most of the Gaels in *The Poor Mouth* know no English. Indeed, many English-speaking visitors to Corkadoragha are careful not to speak English while there, "lest, it seemed, the Gaels might pick up an odd word of it as a protection against the difficulties of life" (48).

14. See also my discussion elsewhere of the possibilities of similar strategies in women's discourse in "'Nothing that is so is so'."

15. Stallybrass and White discuss the importance of pigs as "symbolically base and abject animals," much like rats (5).

Lucky are as familiar in the mythology of the Irish landlord class as they were in that of the plantation owner in the Old South. (53)

The census episode in *The Poor Mouth* points to the potential doubleness of stereotypical associations like that between pigs and peasants. Such mechanical and overly simplistic modes of thought may reinforce the oppression of the Gaels, but they also make the English census taker especially vulnerable to confidence games like that perpetrated by the Old-Fellow. Because the inspector already thinks of the Gaels as pigs, it is quite easy to convince him that the pigs are Gaels.

O'Brien's "talking" pigs function to some extent as carnivalesque images that overturn the social hierarchy that would associate Gaels with pigs and animality.[16] This appropriation of a degrading stereotype has much to do with Rushdie's notion of "reclaiming language from one's opponents." Indeed, this willing association of themselves with pigs has much in common with the strategy of the prophet Mahomet in *The Satanic Verses,* who elects to adopt and to bear proudly a disparaging name hurled at him by his detractors:

> Here he is neither Mahomet nor MoeHammered; has adopted, instead, the demon-tag the farangis hung around his neck. To turn insults into strengths, whigs, tories, Blacks all chose to wear with pride the names they were given in scorn; likewise, our mountain-climbing, prophet-motivated solitary is to be the medieval baby-frightener, the Devil's synonym: Mahound. (93)

But if dominant groups cannot completely prevent their language from containing echoes that are counter to their wishes, then it is also true that the linguistic strategies adopted by marginal groups are similarly susceptible to the production of dialogic counter-currents. Rushdie's "Mahound" adopts that designation in proud defiance of his enemies, yet certain Islamic fundamentalist leaders have taken the label so literally that this renaming of the Prophet has become a central factor in their decision to declare that Rushdie must die for having produced such a blasphemous book. Similarly, marginal groups that would openly em-

---

16. Stallybrass and White mention various examples of carnivalesque literature (such as Ben Jonson's *Bartholemew Fair*) that feature pigs as central images, such that "[i]deological combat is enjoined around the pig which becomes the site of competing definitions and desires" (63). Elsewhere White, reviewing the uses of pigs as symbols in modern literature by authors such as Thomas Pynchon, concludes that "[w]henever we find people described as pigs, something of this carnivalesque inversion, a world turned upside-down, is being reused and applied" (56–57).

brace—even for subversive reasons—the images of animality projected onto them are in danger of merely reinforcing and confirming those stereotypical projections.

Rushdie himself dramatizes this possibility in *The Satanic Verses* with his depiction of Saladin Chamcha. Chamcha is an Indian who has so thoroughly accepted certain British stereotypes of Indian cultural inferiority that he spends most of his life trying to look, act, and sound British rather than Indian. He has moved to London, married an aristocratic British woman, changed his name, changed his voice, even changed his face in order to try to fit in better in Britain.[17] But Chamcha cannot escape his Indian heritage. Having accepted characterizations of Indians as uncivilized and animal-like, he spends most of *The Satanic Verses* in the throes of a transformation into a devilish goat-like beast—literally living out the stereotype. At one point the half-goat Chamcha enters a surrealistic hospital filled with similarly hybrid creatures. One of them, a "Manticore" (a half man–half tiger creature borrowed from Borges), explains how such transformations into animality come about: "They describe us. . . . That's all. They have the power of description, and we succumb to the pictures they construct" (*Satanic* 168). This statement has a special resonance for Chamcha, who has accepted the definitions of Indianness brought about by British Orientalism and has sought to reject all characteristics associated with his homeland.

Likewise, in *The Poor Mouth* it is clear that the Gaels have so thoroughly assimilated stereotypical definitions of Gaelicism that they often accept these offensive characterizations as mechanically as do the English-speaking groups from which the stereotypes arise. It may be that the association with pigs helps to dupe the English language inspector, but it is also true that the Gaels in the book do live in filth and squalor, freely sharing their homes with pigs even at times when there are no inspectors around. When a passing gentlemen suggests to the narrator's family that they erect a little hut outside the house so that they won't have to live with the pigs, they do so. But then the humans move into the hut, leaving the pigs in the house (20).[18]

17. The adopted name "Chamcha" is literally Urdu for "spoon," but also has a second meaning with important resonances concerning Chamcha's Anglophilia. "Colloquially, a *chamcha* is a person who sucks up to powerful people, a yes-man, a sycophant. The British Empire would not have lasted a week without such collaborators among its colonized people" (Rushdie, "Empire" 8). Chamcha's adopted name thus has much in common with the "Jams O'Donnell" of O'Brien's narrator.

18. Compare here Beckett's story "The End," in which the narrator is forced to vacate his apartment so that the landlord's pig can move in. The narrator offers to share his abode with the pig, but is evicted anyway (*Stories* 56).

The excessively literal and unthinking manner in which the family takes this gentleman's advice is characteristic of the behavior of the Gaels in *The Poor Mouth*. The sterile world of Corkadoragha is trapped in an endless cycle of mechanical repetition, its inhabitants perpetually acting out the various stereotypes that have been thrust upon them—and that they have taken upon themselves. The repetitiousness of Gaelic life is emphasized in *The Poor Mouth* by the cyclicity of certain episodes (like the imprisonment of the narrator in the same manner as his father), and also in O'Brien's exaggerated use of the Gaelic language itself, a language that lends itself to rhythmic repetition.[19] Of the several leitmotifs frequently recurring in the book, the most significant is the constant reference to the uniqueness of everyone and everything in the book in various versions of the narrator's central refrain: "I do not think its like will ever be there again." This seemingly-innocent phrase is extremely rich in ironic significance. For one thing, its use in *The Poor Mouth* is a parody of a similar phrase frequently used by Tomás O Criomhthainn in his *An t-Oileánach*.[20] And the phrase is ideally suited for parody, given the irony of using the same words time and again to indicate the impossibility of replication.

The Poor Mouth makes it clear that the likes of the many things whose uniqueness the narrator declares (including himself) will in fact be seen again and again and again. Thus when the narrator and his grandfather arrive in a neighboring village to find it deserted, the boy is confused, but the Old-Fellow knows exactly where the people must be, because their lives always run in the predictable channels of pre-determined narratives:

> 'Tis clear, wee little son, said the Old-Fellow, that you haven't read the good books. 'Tis now the evening and according to literary fate, there's

19. This critique of sterile repetition in Irish life bears certain obvious similarities to Joyce's project in *Dubliners*. Joyce was a major influence on O'Brien's work, and many of Joyce's themes are echoed by O'Brien. However, O'Brien was often highly critical of Joyce, and many of these echoes are reaccentuated in that light. For example, in *Portrait* Stephen criticizes Ireland's resistance to change by characterizing Ireland as "the old sow that eats her farrow" (203). But Dermot Trellis in O'Brien's *At Swim-Two-Birds* is diagnosed as having "an inverted sow neurosis wherein the farrow eat their dam" (314–15).

20. It is, in fact, a favorite Irish cliché. "Big Lambert" of Beckett's *Malone Dies* (a peasant who is, interestingly, a "bleeder and disjointer of pigs") extols his father's uniqueness: "His like will not be seen again . . . once I am gone" (200). Note that Lambert's declaration paradoxically suggests that his father is both unique and very much like himself. Perhaps Lambert's father once said much the same thing about his own father, and so on. On the other hand, the motif is not confined to the Irish. Shakespeare's Hamlet thus says of his dead father that "I shall not look upon his like again."

a storm down on the seashore, the fishermen are in difficulties on the water, the people are gathered on the strand, the women are crying and one poor mother is screaming: Who'll save my Mickey? That's the way the Gaels always had it with the coming of night in the Rosses. (67)

The Gaels of Corkadoragha seem particularly prone to acting out stereotypes, even the literary ones created for them by outsiders. It is thus not surprising that when the "Gaeligores" come from the cities to study authentic Gaelic culture and language, Corkadoragha seems the ideal site for their investigations.[21] At first, this development seems to be another windfall because the Gaeligores have money and can thus stimulate the local economy. In the hope of garnering a few pennies of charity from these Gaeligores, the locals become virtual parodies of themselves, putting their Gaelicism on blatant stereotypical display. Thus, the Gaeligores (who are ostensibly working to preserve and even to revitalize Gaelic culture) serve merely to reinforce prevailing attitudes toward the Gaels as inferior primitives. As Anne Clissmann points out,

> it is in the pathetic willingness of the peasants to live up to the image of Gaelic Ireland created for them by well-fed, well-clothed gentlemen from Dublin that the ridiculous pretensions of the Gaeligores are most exposed. (245)

Again, O'Brien's writing is dialogic, satirizing both the patronizing attitudes of the Gaeligores and the willingness of the Gaels to play up to those attitudes in an attempt to curry favor. But apparently the Gaels of Corkadoragha overdo it a bit, and one by one the Gaeligores leave, discouraged by the fact that local conditions and the local inhabitants are all too typical of Gaelicism, leading to various problems:

1. The tempest of the countryside was too tempestuous.
2. The putridity of the countryside was too putrid.
3. The poverty of the countryside was too poor.
4. The Gaelicism of the countryside was too Gaelic.
5. The tradition of the countryside was too traditional. (50)

The resourceful Old-Fellow realizes that the Gaeligores are leaving because life in Corkadoragha is so unpleasant and comes up with a plan to

21. These Gaeligores are Irish, not English, but they are the clear descendants of Joyce's Englishman Haines, who comes to Ireland to study Gaelic culture in *Ulysses*. Gallagher suggests that the most direct referent of O'Brien's Gaeligores was Synge, for whose romanticizations of the Irish peasant O'Brien felt nothing but contempt (237).

build a local college to house the visiting scholars in conditions that are more amenable to them. In order to raise the money for the college, the Old-Fellow engineers a big Gaelic "feis"—a folk festival attended by country Gaels and city Irishmen alike, very much along the lines of the intermixing of different social groups emphasized by Bakhtin in relation to the carnival.

To Bakhtin, the paradigmatic moment of dialogic cultural interaction occurs during the free intermixture of different social groups in the medieval carnival. But this Gaelic feis is hardly a locus of radical political action. O'Brien's disengaged deadpan narration reinforces the feeling of sterility in this carnival, and the celebration is a virtual disaster for the community. Many of the locals, never too hardy to begin with, lose their health (or even their lives) while working in the rain to construct a speaking platform for use in conjunction with the festivities. Meanwhile, numerous Gaels collapse from hunger and fatigue while listening to the subsequent pompous nonsense that issues forth from the speakers on this same platform. And many others die during various competitions and revels that are held as part of the event. As the narrator notes, "had the feis continued a week longer, no one would be alive now in Corkadoragha in all truth" (61).

Clissmann notes how this feis is "oblivious of the poverty, hunger, and exhaustion of the peasants" (244). The resultant suggestion that a mere festival will not automatically solve these serious social problems speaks directly to the concern that many have expressed over Bakhtin's emphasis on the carnival as a metaphor for the kinds of linguistic interactions that lead to genuine social change. After all, the carnival is an authorized site of transgression, a sanctioned form of "subversion," and one might argue that its very purpose is to sublimate and defuse the social tensions that might lead to genuine subversion—a sort of opiate of the masses. These are important considerations, and O'Brien's sterile feis calls into question some of Bakhtin's more utopian visions of the power of carnival.

However, Bakhtin's work also points toward an explanation of the ineffectiveness of the Gaelic feis in generating new cultural energies. The President of the feis presents a speech that is highly symptomatic of the problems of Gaelic culture in *The Poor Mouth*:

> We are all Gaelic Gaels of Gaelic lineage. He who is Gaelic, will be Gaelic evermore. I myself have not spoken a word except Gaelic since the day I was born—just like you—and every sentence I've ever uttered has been on the subject of Gaelic. If we're truly Gaelic, we must con-

stantly discuss the question of the Gaelic revival and the question of Gaelicism. There is no use in having Gaelic, if we converse in it on non-Gaelic topics. (54)[22]

The extreme cultural solipsism of this speech—the President is so enthralled by Gaelic itself that he ignores the numerous members of his audience who are dropping from hunger as he speaks—indicates that the Gaels are cut off from the kind of genuine political engagement that might be able to inject new energy into their lives. Further, despite his central emphasis on language the speaker does little more here than illustrate the emptiness and sterility of a language that is unable to engage any reality outside of itself—something that O'Brien illustrates elsewhere in meditations on reflexive language like *At Swim-Two-Birds*.

The emphasis on repetition in *The Poor Mouth* also suggests the work of Bakhtin because to Bakhtin pure repetition without re-accentuation is possible only in monologic discourse. No utterance that dialogically interacts with its discursive environment "can ever be repeated; it is always a new utterance (even if it is a quotation)" (*Speech* 108). The repetitive paralysis of Corkadoragha, then, can be imaged as a failure of dialogism, as a surfeit of monologic discourse. Cultural monologism, always anathema to Bakhtin, is generally associated by him with the attempts of dominant groups to impose their own cultural perspectives on society to the exclusion of all others. But in *The Poor Mouth* the marginal Gaelic culture, through its easy acceptance of so many predetermined characterizations of itself, is generally itself quite monologic. To Bakhtin it is in clashes between different cultures and languages that productive dialogue occurs, but the culture of Corkadoragha is pure Gaelic, lacking in the diversity that is necessary for the creation of such dialogue. Without this dialogue, there is nothing to challenge prevailing cultural stereotypes, and the Gaels are trapped in the definitions that both they and their oppressors have perpetrated. Except during rare interactions with outsiders like the language inspector, the Gaels are totally cut off from any meaningful intercourse with other cultures or languages, resulting in the static and stagnating quality of their lives.

O'Brien's description of the sterility of life in Corkadoragha provides a complex multivocal critique of social and cultural conditions in Ireland. On the one hand, it debunks certain romanticized notions of the purity and permanence of life among the Irish peasants that have been accepted

22. Compare the charge of Joyce's Stephen that "you do not care what banality a man expresses so long as he expresses it in Irish" (*Stephen Hero* 54).

and propagated by the peasants themselves.[23] On the other, it suggests that certain big-city "advocates" of Irish peasant culture are only acting to perpetuate stereotypes that contribute to the miserable and deplorable living conditions among real-life Irish peasants. At the same time, the intense emphasis in *The Poor Mouth* on language itself as a locus of cultural definition indicates the powerful way Irish Gaelic peasants have been excluded from mainstream Irish culture by linguistic differences. The preeminence of English-speakers in Irish culture (despite the fact that Gaelic is an officially sanctioned language of the Irish Republic) is a clear echo of centuries of British imperial domination, and O'Brien's implied program for overcoming this domination is a highly Bakhtinian one. But a self-involvement in pure Gaelicism is mere escapism, leaving the Gaels with no means of confronting and challenging the dominant English elements of Irish culture. To O'Brien the hope for genuine social change resides not in the exclusive use of Gaelic or of English, but in the interaction of the two languages to create new effects that break down existing barriers and transcend the status quo. He suggests not that the Irish turn inward to their own culture and ignore outside influences. Rather, he suggests that alien voices (particularly English ones) be appropriated and incorporated into the Irish cultural framework, but that the Irish should resist being overwhelmed by outside influences and by the definitions of Irishness thrust upon them by outsiders. The Irish, in short, should accept freely the British contribution to their culture, acknowledging that contribution with a polite "Thank you, sor."

23. Similar critiques occur in both Joyce and Beckett, the most striking of which is probably Beckett's depiction of the incestuous Lynch clan in *Watt* (100–11).

6

Menippean Energy and Linguistic Subversion
The Hard Life

In *The Hard Life* O'Brien's focus shifts back from Gaelic to English and back from the Irish countryside to the urban setting of Dublin. The novel was first published in 1961, following hard on the "rediscovery" of *At Swim-Two-Birds* that had just brought O'Brien new prominence. *The Hard Life* is set, however, in turn-of-the-century Dublin, its action spanning the period 1890 to 1910. As a result, the Dublin depicted in the book is specifically placed outside the experience of O'Brien himself, who was born in 1911. Indeed, the action is set in a time period that is irresistibly associated—at least in a literary sense—with the work of Joyce. It is not surprising, then, that Joyce will be a powerful presence in *The Hard Life,* and indeed Joycean echoes abound in the text. Clissmann suggests that the book "is an attempt to sum up the atmosphere of *Dubliners* and *A Portrait of the Artist,* with sly digs on the way at *Ulysses.*" In particular, Clissmann argues that *The Hard Life* (as indicated by its subtitle *An Exegesis of Squalor*) parallels Joyce in the "overwhelming evocation of squalor" in its depiction of Dublin (273).

Clissmann is right about the importance of Joyce as an intertextual voice in *The Hard Life.* But, regardless of how oppressive he finds social and political conditions in Dublin, Joyce's texts evoke a far richer "atmosphere" than can be comprehended by "squalor." Joyce's work is particularly rich in the way that he demonstrates the participation of language in the stifling and stultifying cultural climate of Dublin, but at the same time Joyce's exploration of language indicates a latent energy that contains a genuine emancipatory potential. And it is in a similar dialogue with language that *The Hard Life* most importantly engages Joyce's project.[1]

The Hard Life is, like all of O'Brien's work, a book very much about language. One of the ways that it resembles *Dubliners* most is in its evocation of a sterile atmosphere through style as much as content. O'Brien himself described the style of his book as deceptively "pedestrian," a suggestion that recalls the style of "scrupulous meanness" that Joyce sought in *Dubliners*. Further, *The Hard Life* has only a rudimentary plot, and even that is used primarily by O'Brien as a framework within which to conduct various explorations of the use of language. What there is of a plot is itself an extended allusion to Joyce, being based on a Mr. Collopy's dedication to his plan to institute a series of public restrooms for women in Dublin. This plan itself derives in an obvious way from Leopold Bloom's remark as he passes a public urinal for men in *Ulysses* that there "[o]ught to be places for women" (133). O'Brien's conversion of this seemingly insignificant Joycean moment into the plot of an entire novel seems at first to be a purely comic device, in the traditional Irish scatological mode. But Collopy's attitudes, however comical, at least hint at a genuine commentary on the social conditions of women in Ireland. Collopy echoes Bloom in ways other than his concern with urinary convenience, as when he suggests that the women of Dublin suffer from excessive pregnancy, with an unstated implication that the Catholic proscription of birth control contributes to this problem (*Hard* 29).[2]

Moreover, Joyce's passage concerning the urinal is much richer than it might appear. When Bloom sights the urinal he realizes that it is overlooked by a statue of Thomas Moore, at which Joyce's inimitable adman immediately recalls Moore's poem "Meeting of the Waters": "They did right to put him up over a urinal: meeting of the waters" (133). Bloom's

---

1. Mary Power argues that "*The Hard Life* is specifically anti-Joycean and it demonstrates that mythic readings of Irish life are impossible and absurd. . . . O'Brien relentlessly demythologizes Joyce and defines Irish life against idealization of any sort" (89). Power's reading of O'Brien here seems sound, and her article on *The Hard Life* is generally excellent—but her suggestion that Joyce mythologizes and idealizes life in Ireland seems somewhat misguided.

2. Bloom expresses a similar concern at several points in *Ulysses*, especially concerning the travails of Mina Purefoy, whose brutish husband keeps her constantly pregnant. Thus Bloom thinks to himself in relation to the pain of childbirth that "They ought to invent something to stop that" (132). And later, as he visits the lying-in hospital to await Mrs. Purefoy's latest delivery, he muses on "women's woe in the travail that they have of motherhood" (316). Underlying the various dialogues concerning fertility and childbearing in *Ulysses* is a consistent concern with the issue of birth control, which is among other things an important issue in the Blooms's marriage.

ostensibly innocent thoughts are quite frequently charged with significance, and this time is no exception. This jab at Moore, in fact, participates in a motif that occurs several times in Joyce's work. For example,
when Gabriel Conroy debates with himself in "The Dead" over whether
to include a somewhat obscure quotation from Browning in his upcom-
ing postprandial salutation, he wonders if something else might be more
appropriate:

> He was undecided about the lines from Robert Browning for he feared
> they would be above the heads of his hearers. Some quotation that they
> could recognise from Shakespeare or from the Melodies would be bet-
> ter. The indelicate clacking of the men's heels and the scuffling of their
> soles reminded him that their grade of culture differed from his. He
> would only make himself ridiculous by quoting poetry to them which
> they could not understand. (*Dubliners* 179)

In short, Gabriel suggests that the low level of cultural attainment in his
audience will make them unable to understand anything more esoteric
than Shakespeare (to whom presumably everyone has been exposed) and
the *Melodies* of Thomas Moore. This association of Moore with mass
taste is quite consistent with Joyce's use of Moore as a representative of
the degraded state of Irish culture. Moore is mentioned, for example,
among the lowbrow *littérateurs* championed by the old josser in "An
Encounter," and his ballads may be alluded to in the titles of both "Araby" and "Eveline." Gifford sardonically summarizes Moore's literary status by noting that "[n]o properly sentimental Irish home was complete
without its copy of Moore's *Irish Melodies*" (39). Perhaps most importantly, Joyce associates Moore with subservience to the British. In *A Portrait of the Artist as a Young Man* he sarcastically refers to Moore as the
"national poet of Ireland" (180), a label which Gifford suggests has to do
with the way Moore left Ireland for England and "advanced himself by
currying favor in the drawing rooms of the influential in London" (229).

Bloom's suggestion that Moore is quite properly enshrined above a
urinal thus turns out to be a perceptive bit of cultural criticism, satirizing
not only Moore himself, but the taste of an Irish audience that would
accept Moore as a great poet. O'Brien's use of this passage in *Ulysses* to
generate the plot of *The Hard Life* thus partakes of this same cultural
commentary, with a concomitant dash of self-parody that associates his
own work with the same constellation of motifs as Moore's. Meanwhile,
O'Brien's use of *Ulysses* constitutes a potentially subversive parody of the
way Joyce used *The Odyssey* to generate his own plot. The contrast between Joyce's mythic method (centered on an official Great Book of

Western Culture) and O'Brien's (centered on a scatological joke, though one that appears in another Great Book—Joyce's) creates a striking disjunction that calls into question the authority of Great Books in general. On the other hand, Joyce too was subversive in his use of past classics—the only mention of Homer in *Ulysses* is sarcastic, and the main references to Greek culture in *Ulysses* involve Bloom's curiosity over whether the statues of Greek goddesses were anatomically correct.[3]

If the source of O'Brien's plot turns out to be surprisingly significant, his method of presenting that plot is highly significant as well. The plot proceeds not by disclosure and development, but by a process of continual disguise and concealment. We know throughout the text that Collopy is involved in a humanitarian project involving women, but the nature of that project is not revealed until the reading of Collopy's will after his death near the end of the book. Most of what we know comes from the narrator's reinscriptions of the conversations on the topic involving Collopy and the Jesuit Father Fahrt; but as the narrator points out, "the subject under discussion was never named" (27). This strategy is most obviously a spoof of those prudish souls who would find it uncomfortable openly to mention the urinary functions of women, or even to admit that such functions exist—those who are later referred to by Collopy as the "dirty ignoramuses who more or less ban that function" (*Hard* 30). On the other hand, even Collopy and his confederates in this project continually refer to their object of concern by such euphemisms as "it" or "what-you-know." This satire is not unimportant because it suggests that an unrealistic disgust with the physical realities of life makes conditions in Dublin less pleasant, especially for women. It is also highly ironic, given that the text is laced with scatological references, despite the daintiness with which the central topic of women's urination is avoided.[4] It is, in short, silly to attempt to deny that such physical functions exist because all of us participate in them every day of our lives.

But the motif of hidden or missing information inherent in O'Brien's handling of the plot lies very much at the heart of the text and its dialogue with language as well. In *The Hard Life* what is missing is very often at least as important as what is present. At the beginning of the book Finbarr, the book's narrator, reveals that he has never met his father and that when he was five years old his mother died as well. These absent parents suggest another link to Joyce's *Dubliners*, in which parents

---

3. See my discussion of this motif in *Joyce, Bakhtin, and the Literary Tradition*.
4. One thinks here of Dermot Trellis, whose book in *At Swim* is to be a moral tract, but who laces it with pornographic material in order to hold the attentions of his readers.

are quite frequently absent, and in which children are often forced to live with substitutes like uncles and aunts. Finbarr and his brother Manus will also go to live with their uncle Mr. Collopy. But first they undergo a transitional period in which Collopy's daughter Annie comes to care for them in their now-parentless home. The narrator admits that his recollection of this period is probably inaccurate (he was only five at the time), and describes the period as a gap in his life, "a sort of interregum [*sic*], lacuna or hiatus," again pointing to the motif of absence that will remain characteristic of the entire text (12).

Finbarr's characterization of a childhood experience through invocation of these three Latin words also suggests the Greek words "paralysis," "gnomon," and "simony" that so intrigue the boy narrator of "The Sisters." Indeed, the themes of paralysis and simony occur as prominently in *The Hard Life* as they do in *Dubliners,* and the geometric figure of the gnomon (a parallelogram with one corner missing) anticipates the gaps and absences in O'Brien's text quite directly. And the parallel between Joyce's "paralysis, gnomon, simony" and O'Brien's "interregum, lacuna, or hiatus" is indicative of numerous other ways in which "The Sisters" resembles *The Hard Life.* Both texts are similar in their basic depictions of Dublin as a stagnant center of paralysis, though *The Hard Life* has a much more overtly humorous tone. There are more specific parallels as well. For example, the unnamed narrator of "The Sisters," like O'Brien's Finbarr, lives with his uncle in the absence of parents. Both texts thus suggest a basic lack of legitimate authority. In the absence of such authorities, both texts include priests as central figures. But Joyce's Father Flynn is a fallen figure, stricken with a disease that may well be syphilis. And O'Brien's Father Fahrt is an equally ineffective authority figure who seems incapable of anything other than the mouthing of ecclesiastical platitudes and clichés, his speech consisting of little more than the kind of empty passing of wind indicated by his name.

Most importantly, both Joyce and O'Brien see the gaps in legitimate authority that inform their depictions of Dublin as being very much gaps in language itself. The most obvious example of these linguistic absences in *The Hard Life* involves the consistent refusal to name Collopy's project, a refusal that keeps the nature of this project not only from the reader but also from Finbarr and Manus, who frequently witness the conversations of Collopy and Fahrt on this topic. Here again O'Brien echoes "The Sisters," in which various adults consistently speak in a mode of euphemism and circumlocution that allows them to avoid specific mention of key subjects (like sex and death) in the presence of the boy narrator. In particular, Joyce literalizes and calls attention to this motif through the numerous ellipses that punctuate the speeches of the adult characters. For example, Old Cotter attempts to express his suspicions concerning the oddities of Father Flynn in such a way that the adults present will understand his meaning, while the innocent boy will be excluded: "I have my own theory about it, he said. I think it was one of those . . . peculiar cases. . . . But it's hard to say. . . ." (10, Joyce's ellipses). And later, concerning the relationship between the boy and the priest, Cotter notes: "My idea is: let the young lad run about and play with young lads his own age and not be . . . Am I right, Jack?" (10, Joyce's ellipses).

Old Cotter is, apparently, successful in communicating his meaning to Uncle Jack without also communicating that meaning to the boy, who does not understand the conventions of the discourse being spoken sufficiently well to fill in the gaps. The boy does, however, understand that the ellipses contain significant information, and as a result he is greatly troubled by them: "I puzzled my head to extract meaning from his unfinished sentences" (11). In *The Hard Life* this puzzlement largely belongs to the reader, and Thomas F. Shea notes that the reader of *The Hard Life* is similar to the narrator of "The Sisters" in being "perplexed and intrigued by what's not said" (259). That the absences in O'Brien's case constitute an extended slightly-dirty joke, while Joyce's absences point toward much more serious material, does not prevent the two authors from making very much the same point. In both cases, the adult characters continually avoid saying what they mean, and the fact that they can communicate so well even with these gaps in their speech indicates that their language is so conventional and cliché-ridden that large chunks of it can be omitted without any loss in significance.

Joyce frequently demonstrates in his work that the language of Dublin has been reduced to a series of mechanical clichés and empty phrases, indicating the mechanical and empty character of modern Irish life. O'Brien makes a similar point in *The Hard Life*. The conversations of Collopy and Fahrt address this issue in a particularly rich way, going far beyond the realm of Collopy's project into a discussion of a wide range of important issues in Dublin life. There is, for example, a great deal of potential social and political commentary in Collopy's fierce attacks on the municipal authorities of Dublin (referred to locally as the Corporation) for their apparent indifference to his project. In response to Fahrt's suggestion that he might drop a hint to the authorities, Collopy angrily fulminates about the impossibility of getting through to the local officials in Dublin:

> Right well you know that I have the trotters wore off me going up the
> stairs of that filthy Corporation begging them, telling them, ordering

them to do something. I have shown you copies of the letters I have
sent to that booby of a Lord Mayor. That's one man that knows all the
chains, anyhow. What result have I got? Nothing at all but abuse from
cornerboys and jacks in office. (30).

Indeed, Collopy's complaints manage to take in virtually every sector of
the Dublin political climate. Later he mentions that he had considered
enlisting the aid of the Gaelic League, but that they are such
"thooleramawns" that they would no doubt consider his interest in
women's urination prurient and have him arrested (34). And when Fahrt
suggests that Collopy might appeal to Dublin Castle (seat of the lord
lieutenant of Ireland and other British colonial officials) to put pressure
on the Corporation, Collopy again responds that such an appeal would
probably land him in jail, as "those ruffians in the Castle will arrest an
Irishman and charge him with treason if his trousers are a bit baggy or
he forgot to shave" (34–35).

Collopy's complaints thus implicate the municipal authorities of Dublin, the representatives of imperial Britain, and the Irish nationalist opponents of Britain in a sweeping indictment of the indifference of all
political authorities in Ireland to the suffering of the Irish people, especially women. Fahrt, meanwhile, disclaims any interest in politics and
refuses to participate in Collopy's political denunciations, suggesting that
the Catholic Church, that ultimate Irish authority, shows a similar lack of
compassion. Indeed, Fahrt's stance of noninvolvement leads Collopy into
a series of denunciations of the church for its cruelty and indifference. He
suggests, for example, that Fahrt is not concerned about the suffering of
Irish women who lack public facilities because Fahrt and the Church are
in fact all for suffering—as long as they don't have to do it themselves.
When Fahrt suggests that "We are here to suffer," Collopy angrily responds that "You seem to be very fond of suffering when other people
do it" (29). Later, Collopy again attacks Fahrt's "theories in favor of
suffering," associating those theories with Catholicism in general:

> Damn thing you know about suffering yourself. Only people of no ex-
> perience have theories. Of course you are only spewing out what you
> were taught in the holy schools. "By the sweat of thy brow shalt thou
> mourn." Oh the grand old Catholic Church has always had great praise
> for sufferers. (31)

This attack on the apotheosis of suffering in Catholicism echoes one
of Joyce's central complaints about the church. Joyce further suggests in
numerous episodes (like the hellfire and damnation sermon heard by
Stephen Dedalus in *Portrait*) that this emphasis on suffering derives from

a strain of sadism that informs Catholicism in a central way. Perhaps Joyce's most memorable embodiment of this sadism is the brutal Father Dolan, who unjustly pandies the young Stephen at Clongowes Wood. Similarly, the narrator of *The Hard Life* describes his encounters with "the leather" while attending the Catholic Synge Street School, an instrument which

> is nearly as rigid as a club but just sufficiently flexible to prevent the breaking of the bones of the hand. Blows of it, particularly if directly (as often they deliberately were) to the top of the thumb or wrist, conferred immediate paralysis followed by agony as the blood tried to get back to the afflicted part. (22)

The distant tone of this description renders it far less dramatically effective than Stephen's encounter with Baldyhead Dolan, but the similarity between the two texts in this regard is quite obvious.[5]

Collopy's criticisms of Catholicism (and especially the Jesuits) in fact constitute a great portion of his discussions with Father Fahrt, extending into a litany of the various atrocities committed in the name of the church throughout history. At one point he invokes the excesses of the Inquisition, describing them in graphic detail:

> Eight hundred lashes for telling the truth according to your conscience? What am I talking about—the holy friars in Spain propagated the true faith by driving red hot nails into the backs of unfortunate Jewmen. . . . And scalding their testicles with boiling water. . . . And ramming barbed wire or something of the kind up where-you-know. (32)

Collopy also hints at the corruption of the clergy, especially the Jesuits, noting their excessive involvement in various political machinations and in particular their strong concern with material gain:

> Some of the priests mixed up their missionary work with trading and money-making and speculation. A French Jesuit named Father La Valette was up to his ears in buying and selling. Mendicant order my foot. . . . The Order was some class of an East India Company. It was heavenly imperialism but with plenty of money in the bank. (67)

In short, Collopy charges the church with cruelty and sadism, with political maneuvering, with simony, and with being in complicity with

---

5. It should also be pointed out that the consistent irony of *Portrait* suggests that Stephen's reaction to the pandying may in fact be *overly* dramatic, as Stephen's reactions to many things are.

the forces of imperialism—essentially the same charges leveled by Joyce. However, Collopy's anticlerical tirades have a very different flavor from those contained in Joyce's work. In particular, his attacks are extremely attenuated, consisting only of the most stereotypical and clichéd charges. As a matter of fact, they seem to arise less out of a passionate conviction than out of a desire to bait Father Fahrt and to enliven the conversation, as when he praises Martin Luther and the Reformation (32) or when he threatens to turn to the Freemasons for help in his project (35). Thus, Fahrt responds to a series of Collopy's criticisms of the Jesuits by remarking: "You are not serious. You are merely trying to annoy me. You don't believe in what you say at all" (68). In fact, Collopy's charges clearly lack both the passion of some of Stephen Dedalus's anti-Catholic proclamations and the innocence of the anti-Catholic observations of Leopold Bloom.

Almost all of the language in *The Hard Life* is similarly without the backing of any firm conviction. For example, Fahrt's defenses of Catholicism are just as mechanical as Collopy's attacks. His rejoinders to Collopy's arguments consist largely of empty phrases like "You exaggerate," "Oh . . . dear," "I wouldn't say the story is quite so simple as that," and "Hold on a moment now." And even when Fahrt does engage in arguments of his own, his points are largely banal, as when he suggests that the Reformation was inspired by Satan (33), or when he suggests that the best way for Collopy to further his project might be through turning to prayer (36). Indeed, Father Fahrt's discourse seems to consist largely of memorized, prefabricated arguments and quotations, which are further undermined by the fact that his memory is often unreliable. Using information derived from their school studies, Finbarr and Manus sometimes interrupt to correct Fahrt's factual errors, suggesting that Fahrt is drawing on his own past Catholic education, an education that is now too distant to remember with complete accuracy.

All in all, Fahrt's discourse constitutes a far more effective condemnation of Catholicism than does Collopy's. The emptiness and banality with which Fahrt spouts official doctrine suggests that this doctrine is informed by a mechanical repetition that involves no real engagement with the spiritual lives of the people of Ireland. By extension, *The Hard Life* thus suggests that the ongoing power of the Catholic Church in Ireland has more to do with the inability of the Irish to break out of the habits of the past than with any continuing legitimacy of the church as a spiritual authority. The debates of Fahrt and Collopy thus enact the double movement that directs so much of O'Brien's fiction. Even as these debates undermine and criticize the church they also satirize those who would undermine and criticize the church in mechanical and unthinking ways, much in the mode of the confrontations in Flaubert's *Madame Bovary* between the pharmacist Homais and the priest Monsieur Bournisien.[6]

O'Brien's critique of the emptiness of language in Dublin extends beyond Collopy and Fahrt. In particular, Finbarr's brother Manus acts as a sort of linguistic entrepreneur, becoming involved in a number of mail-order enterprise that largely involve the sale of prepackaged discourses. He thus provides a striking literalization of the commodification of language that functions so centrally in O'Brien's work. For example, one of Manus's first projects involves the purchase of 1,500 beautifully bound copies of Cervantes's *Don Quixote* for resale at a profit. The transaction succeeds admirably in a financial sense, but at the expense of reducing Cervantes's great classic to a mere commodity, as the narrator's own description emphasizes:

> They were thick octavo volumes of real beauty in an old-fashioned way, and there were many clear pictures of the woodcut kind. If only as an adornment to bookshelves, they were surely good value for six and six-pence. (57)[7]

Manus next moves into his own publishing enterprise, issuing a series of largely plagiarized pamphlets conveying a variety of prepackaged wisdom. He thus sells language, literally making it a commodity, and it is a language debased not only through plagiarism but through the kind of emptiness that runs through all of the language in *The Hard Life*. Because of the fundamental meaninglessness of all the language marketed by Manus in his various enterprises, he can freely mix widely disparate discourses without any sense of contradiction. Thus, when Manus goes away to London, à la Joyce's Ignatius Gallaher, he sets up the "London University Academy," an institution intended to offer mail-order instruction in everything from archaeology to swimming to the ancient classics to religious vocations. As Manus himself notes in a letter to Finbarr, "We really aim at the mass-production of knowledge, human accomplishment and civilization" (83). In short, the academy is designed to effect a com-

---

6. Note, for example, Bournisien's appeal to "the texts" to substantiate his arguments and Homais's angry reply that "everybody knows that the Jesuits have falsified all texts!" (241).

7. This leveling of all culture to the interchangeability of the commodity is reinforced by Collopy's reaction to *Don Quixote*. He suggests, in ostensible praise, that Cervantes is the "Aubrey De Vere of Spain" (57). De Vere was a nineteenth-century Irish poet of some repute, but by normal standards hardly in the class of Cervantes.

plete commodification of knowledge, reducing it to a mere series of facts that can be mass-marketed in convenient packages.

Manus's educational activities encompass an obvious parody of pedantry, as some of the inserted excerpts from his products indicate. For example, one of his early pamphlets is intended to instruct users walking the high wire, but does so in an academic language that is preposterously "high." It thus begins with a warning: "It were folly to asseverate that periastral peripatesis on the *aes ductile,* or wire, is destitute of profound peril not only to sundry *membra,* or limbs, but to the back and veriest life itself" (40). It then proceeds in the same mode, causing Finbarr to comment that "I do no know what it means and I have no doubt whatever that the brother's "clients" will not know either" (41). And no wonder, because this stilted discourse means virtually nothing. But O'Brien's depiction of Manus extends beyond pedantry to satirize the philistinism of modern Ireland, in which material wealth is valued above spiritual elevation and in which discourses like philosophy, religion, and art are employed not for enlightenment but for purely instrumental purposes in the quest for profit.[8] This attack on philistinism is further enhanced by Manus's own apparent lack of any real human feeling. For example, he feels no compunction whatsoever when a local youth is seriously injured while trying to put into practice his advice on walking the high wire, or even when Collopy is grotesquely killed in an accident that results directly from having consumed the "Gravid Water" supplied by Manus as a remedy for Collopy's rheumatoid arthritis.

Manus treats human beings very much in the same way that he treats everything else—as mere objects, or commodities. Thus, when he hears that the girl Annie may be consorting with bad types, he is concerned not for her moral or emotional health, but merely that she might be in danger of contracting a venereal disease. He responds to the knowledge of Annie's behavior with a long letter to Finbarr in which he describes various graphic symptoms of venereal diseases and suggests that Finbarr be on the lookout for their occurrence in Annie. He thus converts Annie into a purely depersonalized case study. And he continues this objectification of Annie at the book's end when he learns that Annie will have

8. One might compare here the well-known critique of the Enlightenment put forth by Horkheimer and Adorno in *Dialectic of Enlightenment.* They argue that Enlightenment science is precisely characterized by this kind of interest only in information for practical application at the expense of any real understanding, leading to the use of knowledge for the purely instrumental purpose of dominating nature. Importantly, they suggest that this mindset also leads to a mode of human interaction informed primarily by the same drive for domination.

a comfortable regular income as a result of her inheritance from the recently deceased Collopy and suggests that perhaps Finbarr should consider marrying Annie as a source of cash.

This thoroughly unromantic treatment of marriage provokes a strong response from Finbarr, who ends the book with "a tidal surge of vomit," though it is unclear whether the strength of this reaction results from a revulsion at Manus's unscrupulous suggestion or from a horror at the thought of being married to Annie, or both (126). In any case, Manus's impersonal view of marriage is not that far removed from the personal experiences of both himself and Finbarr, who grew up in a household where the spouses Mr. Collopy and Mrs. Crotty hardly acknowledged one another's existence and spoke to each other in only the most formal and ritual and ritualistic ways.[9] And Manus's attitude toward marriage as just another business also again links him to Ignatius Gallaher, who suggests in Joyce's story "The Little Cloud" that if he ever marries it will be not for love, but for money: "If it ever occurs, you may bet your bottom dollar there'll be no mooning and spooning about it. I mean to marry money. She'll have a good fat account at the bank or she won't do for me" (81).

One of Joyce's most telling condemnations of the state of marriage in Dublin occurs in his story "The Boarding House," which treats marriage as a form of prostitution, with Mrs. Mooney playing the role of procuress in the marketing of her own daughter. Indeed, the young men residing in Mrs. Mooney's boarding house refer to her as "The Madam," and Mrs. Mooney views her daughter's relationship with Bob Doran in highly economic terms, with marriage being viewed as a direct alternative to a monetary settlement:

> Some mothers would be content to patch up such an affair for a sum of money; she had known cases of it. But she would not do so. For her only one reparation could make up for the loss of her daughter's honour: marriage. (65)

Polly herself, a clear descendant of Shakespeare's Ophelia, is so thoroughly inscribed within the conventions of Dublin society that she is unable to see that she is being marketed like a prostitute. Like Eveline Hill's, Polly's only alternatives are subjugation to a domineering parent and subjugation to a husband who will probably feel so trapped in the

9. There are, in fact, hints that Mr. Collopy and Mrs. Crotty might not be married at all, which would explain the difference in their names. But Finbarr dismisses this possibility immediately as unthinkable in the moral climate of Catholic Dublin (18).

marriage that he will treat her badly. Either way, she is positioned as an object within the desires of others, having little hope of independently constituting herself as a subject in her own right. *The Hard Life*, on the other hand, contains no direct associations between marriage and prostitution, though it does hint at a possible connection. For example, Manus's suggestion that Finbarr might marry Annie as a source of income resonates with the fact that Finbarr apparently first considers Annie as a sexual being on the night that he observes her lingering with some "young blackguards" in a quarter that "was haunted by prostitutes of the very lowest cadres, and also by their scruffy clients" (90). That Finbarr's adolescent recognition of the existence and importance of sexuality would be associated with prostitutes echoes directly the experiences of Stephen Dedalus, but it also recalls the treatment of marriage as prostitution in "The Boarding House."

O'Brien's treatment of gender issues (which seems rather sophomoric in the light of its central emphasis on Collopy's project for the relief of women) takes on a new seriousness when read through the optic of Joyce. Annie, for example, is very much in the same position as Joyce's Eveline, and no doubt the questionable characters with whom she hangs out have much in common with Eveline's Frank. In *The Hard Life* we never see Annie's point of view—she is merely an impersonal presence in the Collopy household, employed primarily as a servant for her father and nephews. But her domestic situation is very much that of Eveline, through whom Joyce dramatizes the intensely limited nature of the roles available to women in Dublin. In Joyce's story, however, we have access to Eveline's reaction to this stifling situation. Like so many characters in *Dubliners*, Eveline develops fantasies of escape, fantasies that are spurred by a light opera, *The Bohemian Girl*. Importantly, the boys of the earlier *Dubliners* stories identify with and hope to emulate certain heroic models, but the girl Eveline has no such models available. In *The Bohemian Girl*, it is not the girl who is heroic, but Thaddeus, the noble exile who saves her.[10] And so Eveline likewise waits passively for a male savior, in particular the somewhat questionable Frank—an apparent forerunner of the memorable D. B. Murphy of *Ulysses*.

Eveline's visions of transcendent escape parallel those of the boys in the earlier stories quite directly. She will escape to exotic Buenos Ayres [*sic*], where she will find true love and happiness. But, importantly, she is

10. See Kershner for a fuller discussion of the relevance of this opera to the story (*Joyce* 63–65).

unable to develop a heroic image of herself, depending instead on Frank to supply the heroism required to effect her salvation:

> Escape! She must escape! Frank would save her. He would give her life, perhaps love, too. But she wanted to live. Why should she be unhappy? She had a right to happiness. Frank would take her in his arms, fold her in his arms. He would save her. (40)

As a young woman in Dublin, Eveline cannot act; she can only react. In the end, she turns away from Frank and remains with her father, but of course it makes little difference. Thoroughly trapped as an object within male fantasies and unable to establish any vision of her own self-hood outside those fantasies, Eveline will be equally dominated whether she stays or goes. So she remains within the dominion of her father, despite her loss of any belief that he merits such loyalty, just as Joyce's Dubliners all remain inscribed within discourses of power that have no real justification or legitimacy.

Clearly, O'Brien's Annie is trapped in very much the same way that Joyce's Eveline is trapped. It thus might be a serious abuse of Annie were Finbarr to marry her for her money, but in general it would be an extension of the way she has been treated all her life, and she will probably remain in very much the same position whether Finbarr marries her or not. Any marriage she makes is unlikely to bring her genuine fulfillment, as marriage—like other potential sources of spiritual and emotional growth in the Dublin of *The Hard Life*—is a degraded institution that echoes the degraded condition of Irish life in general. Moreover, if one links O'Brien's treatment of Annie and of marriage to Joyce, one finds a potentially serious dialogue with other issues raised by *The Hard Life* as well. For example, Joyce specifically links his critique of marriage to his ongoing assault on Catholicism, consistently suggesting in *Dubliners* that marriage is a principal means through which the church exerts its hegemony over the lives of the Irish people. Both marriage and the church should be sources of hope, inspiration, and true intersubjective connection, but in Joyce's Dublin both merely contribute to the atmosphere of spiritual sterility and paralysis.

The implications of this treatment of marriage are significant in both *The Hard Life* and *Dubliners*. Michel Foucault notes in his description of the rise of marriage in social importance during the time of the Roman Empire that the relationship of a man to his wife came to be regarded as a model of respectful relationship with the Other:

> In the conjugal bond that so strongly marks the existence of each person, the spouse, as privileged partner, must be treated as a being identical to oneself and as an element with whom one forms a substantial identity. . . . The woman as spouse is valorized . . . as the other par excellence. (*Care* 163–64)

For Foucault this respectful treatment of one's wife is part of the technologies of the self through which one develops a suitable selfhood of one's own. And though the rise of Christianity initiated numerous changes in the role of marriage, the spousal relation remained the epitome of mutual intersubjective relation in Western society. The degraded condition of marriage in *Dubliners* and *The Hard Life,* where conjugal partners show an almost total lack of mutual affection, respect, or communication, thus stands not only as an image of the degraded form of religious institutions in general but as a sign of the way self-constitution through mutual intersubjective relation almost invariably fails in Dublin. The Dublin citizenry is so accustomed to a society structured around domination and submission that they interact with one another on a similar basis, leaving them incapable of any effective cooperative action to improve the miserable conditions of their lives.

For both Joyce and O'Brien, the impossibility of successful creative self-constitution through marriage is only one aspect of the general inability of the citizens of Dublin to develop positive and dynamic images of themselves. In *Dubliners* and *The Hard Life* parents are either missing or ineffectual, governmental authorities are corrupt and incompetent, the church is selfish and indifferent. The society in general suffers from a severe dearth of positive role models; and when there is a potential hero (like Charles Stewart Parnell), the society strikes him down. One might, of course, argue that the scrupulous meanness with which both *Dubliners* and *The Hard Life* are presented merely contributes to this problem, and the recognition by both Joyce and O'Brien that they are themselves part of the Dublin culture they criticize no doubt accounts at least in part for the prevalence of self-parody in both writers.

Dubliners, however, is paradoxically rich. "The Dead" especially points toward possible alternatives to the paralysis of Dublin culture. Even if critical suggestions that Gabriel Conroy undergoes an experience of genuine spiritual transcendence in this story do not really seem consistent with the story, the lyrical style of "The Dead" represents a significant departure from the style of scrupulous meanness informing the other stories, suggesting the beginnings of an awakening from paralysis. In this sense, then, the final *Dubliners* story does in fact represent a potential

move toward a correction to the lack of meaningful intersubjective relationship afflicting the populace of Dublin. And even if the characters in
earlier stories like "The Sisters" seem unable to speak in anything but
clichés, they also continually undermine themselves with slips and inadvertent puns which suggest that language itself contains a richness and a
power that presents an imaginative potential, even if the characters themselves are devoid of imagination.[11]

The language of *The Hard Life* has a similar potential, even if that
potential has not been widely acknowledged. For example, Shea argues
that the book only "masquerades" as a realistic novel and that it in fact
"explores how discourses collapse, sounding only a desperately squalid
void" (258). Shea's reading is important in its recognition of the reflexive
focus on language that lies at the heart of *The Hard Life,* but even Shea
sees this focus as a primarily negative demonstration of the emptiness
and futility of language in modern Dublin. He notes that Collopy laces
his speech with Irish expressions like "pishrogues," "gobshite," and
"smahan," arguing that such expressions are unauthentic and that they
demonstrate the lack of any real energy in his language (260). Granted,
Collopy is hardly an ideal representative of Irish national pride, but he
does show a clear resentment against the British imperial domination of
the Ireland of his time. Early in the book he notes the tendency of the
inhabitants of Bull Island to adopt the latest British fashions (like playing
golf) and angrily remarks that "We're as fit for Home Rule here as the
blue men in Africa if we are to judge by those Bull Island looderamawns"
(17). Late in the book Collopy goes to Rome and meets the pope, who
asks him if things are going well in Ireland. "Only middling, Your Holi-
ness," he responds. "The British are still there" (109).

In this light, it is possible to read Collopy's Irishisms as an expression of protest, however feeble, against the British linguistic domination
of Ireland. In this case, O'Brien's decision to situate the book in the
British colonial period might be highly significant, the suggestion being
that much of the linguistic domination associated with the British colonization of Ireland may still be relevant within the cultural context of the
Irish Free State. One thinks here again of Salman Rushdie and his project of "decolonizing" English, especially because Rushdie himself specifically cites O'Brien as an important predecessor. It is certainly true that
Collopy's discourse has less energy than what Gerald Marzorati calls "the
lustrous, alloyed English . . . fused from street slang, Great Books, rock

---

11. I discuss this aspect of "The Sisters" in some detail in "History and Language in
Joyce's 'The Sisters'."

songs, ad jingles, immigrant patois, *everything*" (27, his emphasis) that Rushdie employs, but that may be largely the point. O'Brien depicts a language that is expressly lacking in energy, a language nearly squashed beneath the weight of centuries of imperial domination, yet one could certainly argue that Collopy's Irish expressions indicate a small glimmer of resistance, even as they indicate the difficulty (and possible inauthenticity) of such resistance. Thus, in keeping with his consistently dialogic mode of satire, O'Brien uses Collopy to strike a blow at the British while at the same time undermining Collopy himself.

This double movement suggests precisely the kind of dialogic discourse privileged by Bakhtin, and again points toward the way *The Hard Life* can be read in connection with the tradition of Menippean satire.[12] Indeed, the book contains numerous Menippean elements, including carnivalesque mixtures of disparate discourses, scatological imagery, elements of the fantastic, and satire of specific ideas and attitudes. Despite its realist surface, the book shows many of the same signs of heteroglossic bricolage construction as does *At Swim-Two-Birds*. Clissmann finds *The Hard Life* unsatisfying because "it lacks coherence and is too one-sided a vision of squalid reality" (290). However, the book may not be quite as one-sided as it first appears, and indeed it may be the very multiplicity of voices in the text that leads Clissmann to find that it lacks coherence. The polyphonic texture of a Menippean text always lacks a certain coherence, but only because of the plurality of the various languages embedded in the text. And the Menippean clash of discourses that occurs in *The Hard Life* has the potential to release powerful subterranean energies that contradict the deadly monotonous quality of the book's surface.

The very fact that so many different discourses are mixed together in the text (as in the radically multidisciplinary curriculum of Manus's London University Academy) already indicates a certain potential for productive dialogue. But, most importantly, *The Hard Life* frequently effects the kind of juxtaposition of the "low" and the "high" that is the central characteristic of the Menippean carnival. Manus's academy does indeed represent a devaluation of human knowledge, but it is significant that this project encompasses a gamut of subjects that ranges from ostensibly sublime areas like "Ancient Classics" and "Religious Vocations" to the abjection of areas like "Prevention and Treatment of Boils" (82). The

12. Mary Power usefully places the book in the tradition of classical Juvenalian satire as well, but the inherently multigeneric nature of Menippean satire makes it easy for the book to participate in both satiric traditions.

resultant suggestion that such widely disparate subjects can be treated in much the same way indicates a commodification of knowledge, but it also potentially challenges traditional cultural hierarchies in ways that might be highly productive. In particular, this juxtaposition undermines the claims of discourses like art and religion that they are superior to the "lower" realm of the physical.

The Hard Life consistently effects a Rabelaisian juxtaposition of excremental imagery with presumably lofty spiritual ideas. Clissmann notes (apparently as a criticism of the book's lack of profundity) that "the comedy of *The Hard Life* stems from its concentration on the basic functions of man set side by side with his intellectual pretensions" (280). Importantly, however, foremost among these "intellectual pretensions" in *The Hard Life* is the claim of the Catholic Church to moral and spiritual leadership in Ireland. For example, the book's subtitle indicates a juxtaposition of the religious (exegesis) with the filthy (squalor) of a kind that is of central importance to the text. Like Beckett and Joyce, O'Brien frequently uses the church as a symbolic focus for his satiric attacks on bureaucratic corruption and intellectual inauthenticity. Because of its central place in Irish culture and society, the church becomes for all of these Irish writers a central instance of the kinds of bogus "official" and "high" culture that they consistently attack in their work. In *The Hard Life* O'Brien's dialogic confrontations between the "purity" of Catholicism and the "dirtiness" of sex and excrement suggest in a highly subversive way that Catholicism as an institution is in fact informed by a fascination with the very kinds of physical processes that it purports to reject.[13] The book (like much of O'Brien's work) thus vividly enacts the suggestion of Stallybrass and White that the drive toward "exclusion of filth" on the part of official society is often merely a disguise for an intense interest in such "filth": "disgust always bears the imprint of desire. These low domains, apparently expelled as 'Other', return as the object of nostalgia, longing and fascination" (Stallybrass and White 191).

O'Brien's subtle association of the church with "filth" inheres particularly in his depiction of Father Fahrt, an ambassador of spirituality who is frequently associated in *The Hard Life* with the physical. When we first meet Fahrt he is scratching frantically at his back due to an apparent attack of psoriasis. And later we find Fahrt indulging in the physical pleasures of both tobacco and alcohol. But the rejection of the physical by the church is satirized most vividly in the scene late in *The Hard Life*

13. On a similarly carnivalesque treatment of religion in Joyce and Beckett (and Thomas Pynchon), see my essay "The Rats of God."

when Collopy appeals directly to the pope for help in his project to construct public toilet facilities for Dublin's women. Our access to this encounter, which turns out to be one of the most hilarious in the book, is actually fourth-hand—Finbarr relays it to us from a letter he receives from his brother Manus, who was at the meeting in Rome; but Manus was unable to hear most of Collopy's remarks or to understand the pope's Latin and Italian, so he had to rely on the later translation of the pope's remarks by a Monsignor Cahill, while Collopy's statements remain lost entirely. The indirect and partial nature of the transcription of this papal audience resonates with the motif of missing information that runs through the rest of the text, especially as Collopy's description of his project is absent and the pope's angry reaction—which suggests a lack of interest of the pope in the problems of women—does not indicate the nature of what he is reacting against. Moreover, the juxtaposition of English, Italian, and Latin in this scene effects a heteroglossic mixture of the various languages of Stephen Dedalus's (and Ireland's) "two masters" (*Ulysses* 17), with the native Gaelic language of the Irish (including Collopy's feeble echoes of that language) being conspicuous by its absence. This conversation, for all its humor, thus enacts both the suppression of Ireland by foreign forces and the suppression of physicality by Catholicism.

Collopy dies in a grotesque accident soon after his papal interview; and as a final addition to this juxtaposition of Catholicism with urination, O'Brien has Collopy leave money in his will for the establishment of a series of three public facilities for women to be named after the Saints Patrick, Jerome, and Ignatius. Shea suggests that this final bequest once again shows Collopy's clumsiness with language because this naming will probably discourage women from using the facilities (266). Indeed, as a practical project this naming strategy has severe problems. But as a literary crowning touch it is highly appropriate. It is only here at the end of the book that we learn the nature of Collopy's project and can therefore connect it to the recommendation of Leopold Bloom in *Ulysses*. And Collopy's association of these saints with the urinals immediately links up with Bloom's thoughts about Thomas Moore to suggest that Collopy in fact "did right" to name the urinals after Catholic saints as final carnivalesque subversion of the pretensions of Catholicism.

Odds are that Collopy himself would not be aware of the carnivalesque implication of his scheme for naming his rest rooms—after all, he could not be alluding to *Ulysses* if he died in 1910. This final act of irreverence toward such prominent saints thus suggests a subversive power in language itself that exceeds individual intention. It also suggests that even the ostensibly "pedestrian" style of *The Hard Life* still shows a concern with language of a kind that belies the usual picture of O'Brien as a writer who gradually turned away from the reflexive concerns that so centrally inform *At Swim-Two-Birds*. This last conflation of the saintly with the excremental also continues the consistent strain of subversion of figures of authority that runs through O'Brien's writing.

7

O'Brien's Final Critique of Authorities
The Dalkey Archive

In a letter to Timothy O'Keefe (November 15, 1963), Flann O'Brien explained of *The Dalkey Archive:* "The book is not meant to be a novel or anything of the kind but a study in derision, various writers with their styles, and sundry modes, attitudes and cults being rats in the cage" (cited in Clissmann 293). O'Brien's description provides a useful perspective on his book, clearly placing it, with all of his other major works, within the tradition of the Menippean satire. *The Dalkey Archive* is an extended assault on monologism, mastery, and authoritarianism—precisely the sort of project for which Bakhtin praises the Menippean spirit. In the book O'Brien trots out an impressive array of figures of scientific, religious, secular, and literary authority, undercutting them all while at the same time undermining the pretensions to mastery of the central character Mick Shaughnessy, and finally (though perhaps unintentionally) of himself as author.

Such critiques of mastery and authority have a special resonance in the work of Irish writers, who have enjoyed an astonishing ascendancy in twentieth-century "English" literature, while consistently focusing on themes of futility and showing a skeptical attitude about the mastery of the Irish artist and of artists in general. Writers like Joyce, Beckett, and O'Brien participate in this trend in a central way, though each of these three writers has his own special perspective on Irish culture. All of Joyce's stay in Ireland occurred during a period of British rule, while independence for most of Ireland was gained relatively early in the lives of O'Brien and Beckett, a generation younger. Joyce and O'Brien were Irish Catholics, whereas Beckett came from a Protestant background.

105

Both Joyce and Beckett left Ireland at relatively early ages, remaining exiles, while the long-time civil servant O'Brien lived his entire life in his native country. Perhaps most importantly, O'Brien and Beckett had Joyce as a predecessor. Indeed, the dialogue between art and authoritarianism takes an interesting self-reflexive turn when one considers the extreme importance of the work of Joyce to successors like Beckett and O'Brien. Joyce's attacks on mastery were so seemingly masterful that he himself has often been seen as a new authority in his own right. Both Beckett and O'Brien had more in common with Joyce throughout their careers than has been perceived by most critics, but it is also true that both Beckett and O'Brien waged their campaigns against mastery partially by seeking to evade the Joycean shadow. It comes as no surprise, then, that Joyce himself figures as one of the principal images of authority who are parodied in *The Dalkey Archive,* perhaps one of the most sustained attacks on mastery in modern literature.

In the book's opening pages Mick and his friend Hackett come upon a slightly injured man they help back to his home. This man, De Selby (a reinscription of the de Selby of *The Third Policeman*), turns out to be a sort of mad scientist who has invented a substance known as D.M.P., which extracts oxygen from the air, with the express purpose of effecting the extinction of all life on earth.[1] De Selby's apocalyptic vision is most directly a commentary on the way science's attempts to master life have led to the development of a technology that threatens to end life altogether. As such, *The Dalkey Archive* belongs to a family of post-World-War-II works that are centrally informed by the reality of the threat of nuclear holocaust, like Beckett's *Endgame* and Thomas Pynchon's *Gravity's Rainbow*. But the depiction of De Selby makes the more general point that life itself is inimical to mastery. The contingency of life in the real world involves an element of chance and of sheer disorderliness that escapes all of humanity's best efforts to enclose it in masterful systems of explanation. In life, as Wallace Stevens puts it, "the squirming facts exceed the squamous mind" (215).

That De Selby's denial of life is in fact a general property of human systems of mastery and not just of science is emphasized by the fact that De Selby's arcane researches extend into the realms of philosophy and theology as well. De Selby himself emphasizes the multidisciplinary nature of his work: "Call me a theologian or a physicist as you will," he

1. That these initials also suggest the Dublin Municipal Police is, of course, not accidental, suggesting that the police (and official authority in general) have a suffocating effect on life in Dublin.

tells Mick and Hackett, "but I am serious and truthful" (18). De Selby's firm resolution to rid the planet of all life illustrates the fierce incompatibility between neat systems of abstraction (like science, religion, or philosophy) and life as it actually is, with all its messiness and contingency. De Selby makes quite clear his objection to the abject reality of physical existence:

> It merits destruction. Its history and prehistory, even its present, is a foul record of pestilence, famine, war, devastation and misery so terrible and multifarious that its depth and horror are unknown to any one man. Rottenness is universally endemic, disease is paramount. The human race is finally debauched and aborted. (19)

Yet even De Selby's attempts to negate the disease and decay of real life cannot escape the aleatory elements of that life. In the course of developing the agent D.M.P. he discovers that it not only removes oxygen from the air but also has the entirely accidental side effect of suspending the passage of time. With the clear intent of commenting upon philosophers of time like Newton, Spinoza, Bergson, Descartes, and Einstein (and perhaps upon Aristotle's view of time as movement), De Selby suggests that all such theories are bogus and that time is in fact an illusion (14–15).

De Selby's ability to suspend time represents the realization of the standard aestheticist's dream of escaping temporality and moving into an eternal world of art. Such a vision has often been associated with modernism in general (like in Joseph Frank's meditations on "spatial form"), but it is also a vision that frequently occurs in modern Irish letters, as in Wilde's "Critic as Artist" or *The Picture of Dorian Gray,* or in poems like Yeats's "Sailing to Byzantium." Perhaps the Irish artist most associated with such a vision is Stephen Dedalus, and much of O'Brien's critique of such attempts to escape temporality can be read as an implicit critique of Stephen's privileging of "the luminous silent stasis of esthetic pleasure" (*Portrait* 213). Joseph Buttigieg illuminates this vision:

> At the very center of Stephen's aesthetic vision lies the ideal of stasis, the antithesis of temporality. When he elaborates on his idea of stasis, Stephen reveals the distrust he shares with Hulme of anything suggestive of the body and its appetites. (72)[2]

2. For years, it was common in Joyce criticism to attribute this aestheticist attitude to Joyce himself. Interestingly, J. C. C. Mays correctly disputes this view of Joyce, noting the "populist" and "egalitarian" nature of Joyce's art. But then Mays promptly suggests that it

This distrust of the body and its appetites is mirrored in De Selby's disgust with all things physical as embodiments of disease and decay. This rejection of the physical has much in common with Catholic tradition as well, and the Catholic Church is one of the principal representatives of mastery and authority that are parodied in *The Dalkey Archive*. Midway through the book Mick decides to employ the Jesuit Father Cobble (a descendant of Father Fahrt of *The Hard Life*) to engage De Selby in theological discussions in order to distract the scientist while Mick devises a plan to keep him from destroying the world. Mick does not explain to the Jesuit the nature of De Selby's project, but he does suggest to De Selby and Father Cobble that they might have much in common because the former is trying to find a way to disseminate his D.M.P. substance around the globe, while the latter is charged to do the same with the Christian faith (122). The implied suggestion that spreading Christianity is akin to spreading a substance that destroys all life is apparent to the reader, though it is understandably lost on Father Cobble. And the priest's reply provides a prophetic anticipation of the contemporary world of American TV evangelism:

> Modern achievements in radio and television, tape recording and all the magic of the cinema have so radically improved communication—*communication*, I repeat—that the old-fashioned preacher going into the wilds is now almost obsolete. Beside the pulpit we may now place the microphone. (123)

Father Cobble, a rather heavy drinker who is described as a "nonentity" (127), provides only a minor target for the critique of mastery in *The Dalkey Archive*. O'Brien does, however, have bigger religious game in his sights in the person of the church father St. Augustine. Indeed, Augustine is the ideal target because he was one of the philosophical founders of the Catholic revulsion with the physical and because he was also centrally concerned with meditations on the contrast between time and eternity. In fact, Augustine anticipates De Selby's view of time as human illusion when in Book XI of his *Confessions* he suggests that the past exists merely as a product of human memory, while the future exists merely as a product of human expectation. From the point of view of

---

is O'Brien who is the aesthete: "Joyce's achievement comes to rest on human qualities . . . [but] O'Nolan's range—though it defines itself as a critique of Joyce the artist—comes increasingly to rest on qualities of pure artistry" (249). But O'Brien's work elsewhere (as in the *Cruiskeen Lawn* newspaper columns he wrote as Myles na gCopaleen) shows a strong appreciation for contemporary popular culture that underscores a contempt for aestheticism (see Clissmann 230–31).

God, all times exist simultaneously, precisely the situation produced by De Selby's D.M.P.

De Selby offers to demonstrate the time-stopping powers of D.M.P. to Mick and Hackett by using it to produce a personage from history, who will be brought into the present. That worthy turns out to be none other than Augustine himself, though it is a rather peculiar version of Augustine who speaks with an "unmistakable" Dublin accent, and who even suggests that the famous debauchery of his youth might have been brought about by "the Irish in me" (35).[3] Augustine's Irishness further enhances the link between his antilife philosophy and Irish culture, while his speech also reinforces the connection between a rejection of physicality and a desire to escape temporality. For example, he describes time as "a confusing index of decomposition" (35).

Augustine's discourse parodies religion as an abstract system of imposing order on the universe in much the same way that De Selby's parodies science. Augustine's speech is liberally sprinkled with irreverences and downright blasphemies, many of which are specifically designed to deconstruct the church's traditional opposition between the purity of spirituality and the contamination of physicality. Indeed, the chief administrator of the heaven from which Augustine descends turns out to be a mysterious "Polyarch," whose nature (divine or diabolic) remains indeterminate. De Selby prepares the way for this motif by suggesting that, because the victors write the histories of wars, we cannot be certain that the biblical account of Lucifer's rebellion is accurate. "For if—I repeat *if*—the decision had gone the other way and God had been vanquished, who but Lucifer would be certain to put about the other and opposite story?" (22–23).

Augustine continues his assault on orthodoxy when he mocks Origen, the early church father who castrated himself in order to escape the lures of the flesh, asking "How could Origen be the Father of Anything and he with no knackers on him?" (37). Further, he implicates such pillars of religion as Francis Xavier, Ignatius Loyola, and John Calvin in the physicality of human existence by suggesting that they could have been found "[h]obnobbing and womanising in the slums of Paris . . . in warrens full of rats, vermin, sycophants, and syphilis" (37).

The mention of Calvin suggests that Protestants are not exempt from the critique of religion embodied in Augustine's discussions of the church. It is important to note that St. Ignatius was the founder of the

---

3. This dialogue with the dead Augustine recalls the Menippean tradition of works like Lucian's *Dialogues of the Dead*.

Jesuits and that St. Francis Xavier was a prominent Jesuit himself. Indeed, Augustine goes on to note that "Jesuits are the wiliest, cutest and most mendacious ruffians who ever lay in wait for simple Christians" (38). The Jesuits form ideal targets for O'Brien's assault on mastery because their emphasis on learning allows him to mock both religion and pedantry in a single blow. This emphasis on the Jesuits also suggests an additional parallel with the work of Joyce, in which Jesuits figure so prominently.

Augustine's attacks on the Jesuits also provide a further link between his discourse and that of De Selby, who appears to find Jesuits particularly contemptible. In fact, among the principal faults De Selby finds with Descartes are the latter's solipsism and "liking for the Jesuits" (16). Like De Selby, Augustine disparages Descartes, whose dualistic philosophy embodies precisely the kind of strict separation of the physical and the spiritual that is so thoroughly criticized by *The Dalkey Archive* as a whole. He thus suggests that Descartes stole his famous *cogito ergo sum* from Augustine's own work (42), and it is true that Descartes does here echo Augustine. What this fictional Augustine does not appear to realize, in fact, is that all of the targets of his vituperation have much in common with the historical Augustine, so that his discourse constantly tends to undermine itself. Moreover, though De Selby and Augustine launch similar attacks on the authorities of science and religion respectively, they also tend to attack each other. De Selby explains the silliness of philosophical attempts to capture time within abstract explanatory systems:

> Consideration of time, he said, from intellectual, philosophic or even mathematical criteria is fatuity, and the preoccupation of slovens. In such unseemly brawls some priestly fop is bound to induce a sort of cerebral catalepsy by bringing forward terms such as infinity and eternity. (14)[4]

But terms like "infinity" and "eternity" are precisely what Augustine does bring forward, and it is worth noting too that De Selby specifically mocks the Cartesian cogito for which Augustine later takes credit (15). Finally, the direct dialogue between De Selby and Augustine (35–45)

---

4. Interestingly, Paul Ricoeur has recently reached a somewhat similar conclusion in his far-reaching phenomenological study of time. Ricoeur compares Augustine's treatment of time to those proposed by thinkers ranging from Aristotle to Heidegger and concludes that paradoxes in which such treatments turn back on themselves in logical paradoxes are inevitable. To Ricoeur, the only solution must be a poetic one: "temporality cannot be spoken of in the direct discourse of phenomenology, but rather requires the mediation of the indirect discourse of narration" (241).

often descends into insult and innuendo, with De Selby characterizing Augustine's arguments as incoherent "flannel" (42–43).

The disputation between De Selby and Augustine is particularly ironic in that the two opponents are both arguing from basically similar positions—both are fundamentally concerned with the construction of abstract systems that will allow them to escape the messiness of reality. The result is a suggestion that science, religion, and philosophy are engaged in similar drives toward mastery and domination. Further, O'Brien brings politics into this mix as well. For example, though O'Brien is writing within the context of an Ireland that has been ostensibly free of British rule for forty years, he hints in *The Dalkey Archive* that British domination has still not been completely overcome. When Mick and Hackett see a distant monument just before finding De Selby, they wonder if it might be the statue of some great Irish hero, like Johannes Scotus Erigena or Parnell, but they are wrong: "No indeed: Queen Victoria" (8). And later Mick shows a lingering memory of the years of British political, economic, and religious domination when he reminds a Protestant clergyman that

> this country has for centuries been subjected to vicious overtaxation and exploitation, both by the British Government and a cabal of corrupt and pitiless ruffians called absentee landlords. . . . And I don't offend your reverence, I hope, by bringing to mind the horror of the tithes, when a beggared peasantry were compelled to support a Church in which they had no belief and for which they had no use. (142)

In O'Brien, however, the figures of civil and political authority most consistently satirized are Irish ones. In particular, his work often features huge, bumbling, inept Irish policemen—a phenomenon also seen frequently in the writing of Beckett. One of the principal characters in *The Dalkey Archive* is the inimitable Sergeant Fottrell, the Dalkey police official who spends most of his time stealing bicycles and puncturing tires. But the good sergeant means well, and these acts of vandalism and theft are in fact performed as a public service. For Sergeant Fottrell is also an amateur scientist, and his scientific researches have led him to the discovery of the "Mollycule Theory." Based on the premise that two objects in physical contact will tend to exchange molecules, Fottrell has concluded that the excessive riding of bicycles will eventually lead one to be composed entirely of bicycle molecules, while the bicycle itself will eventually become entirely human. Trying to minimize this phenomenon, Fottrell wages a guerilla campaign to prevent the riding of bicycles in his area.

O'Brien gets a great deal of satiric mileage out of this ludicrous "Mollycule Theory," largely reinscribed from the "Atomic Theory" of *The Third Policeman*. For example, Fottrell shows a typically Irish concern with the repression of sexuality by hinting at the prurient implications of his theory for the case of a man riding a lady's bicycle: "It's the height of sulphurous immorality, the P.P. would be within his rights in forbidding such a low character put as much as his nose inside the church" (92–93).[5] In addition, there is a reminder of the continuing British economic domination of Ireland (and a simultaneous parody of the Irish Nationalist concern with Irish racial purity) in Mick's suggestion of the political consequences of such molecular exchanges between human and bicycle. "All decent Irishmen should have a proper national outlook," he tells Sergeant Fottrell. "Practically any bike you have in Ireland was made in either Birmingham or Coventry." "Yes," responds the sergeant. "There is also an element of treason entailed. Quite right" (95). Fottrell follows with an additional example of the social consequences of his theory, providing an interesting commentary on the Irish system of justice with the story of a Mr. McDadd, who was convicted of murder, but whose bicycle was hung in his place since most of his molecules were in fact in the bicycle (96).

The principal effect of the "Mollycule" passage, however, is to satirize scientific thinking while at the same time suggesting a complicity between the kind of thought embodied in science and that displayed by figures of authority like policemen. Fottrell's theory starts with a kernel of fact (that molecules do move and theoretically can change places in the manner he indicates), but he then carries the theory far beyond this kernel into the realm of the ridiculous. The obvious flaws in Fottrell's theory suggest that science in general may have exceeded reasonable bounds in its attempts to explain the world and to circumscribe it within its neat theoretical constructs.

This attack on science's pretenses to mastery is reinforced later in Mick's conversation at the Colza Hotel with Dr. Crewett and the medical student Nemo Crabbe. Crewett suggests that Fleming's "discovery" of penicillin was in fact merely a formalization of a knowledge that had been available to folk medicine for centuries, the implication being that ethnocentric Western science is not so superior to a variety of alternative modes of thought generally considered to be more "primitive." Crewett explains:

---

5. This motif is developed at more length in *The Third Policeman*, in which Michael Gilhaney's male bicycle seduces a female teacher (89). Moreover, the nameless narrator makes his escape from the police station on a female bicycle, with decidedly sensuous results (173).

That's why it's foolish for men in western Europe to be supercilious about witch-doctors, their brews and decoctions, eye of newt and toe of frog, and so on. Those savages knew nothing of chemistry or pathology but they were capable of carrying on uncomprehended but sound medical traditions. The birds and the brute creation have similar instinctive remedies for their own sicknesses. (109)

Mick, frankly, is not very interested in Crewett's pronouncements on alternative science, but he does come to attention when the doctor casually announces that James Joyce is alive and well (in the early 1960s) at some undisclosed location. Mick then delivers a surprisingly accurate assessment of Joyce's work:

I consider his poetry meretricious and mannered. But I have an admiration for all his other work, for his dexterity and resource in handling language, for his precision, for his subtlety in conveying the image of Dublin and her people, for his accuracy in setting down speech authentically, and for his enormous humour. (111)[6]

Mick decides to set out in search of Joyce so that some of the errors made by critics of Joyce's work (another group whose pretensions to mastery are thus parodied) can be corrected. In fact, Mick easily locates Joyce, who is now an old man working at a tavern in the small Irish resort town of Skerries. Early in the writing of *The Dalkey Archive* O'Brien wrote of Joyce in a letter to Gerald Gross that "I'm going to get my own back on that bugger" (cited in Clissmann 291). And indeed the portrait of Joyce given in the book is highly satiric—we find this Joyce a greatly diminished figure, rabidly pious, whose only dream is to somehow become a Jesuit despite his advanced age.

Joyce thus becomes another of the figures of mastery who are ridiculed by O'Brien's book. In particular, Joyce's exalted authorial status is diminished by his own protestations that of the work attributed to him he actually wrote only *Dubliners,* which he coauthored with his friend Gogarty. O'Brien's Joyce seems not to have even heard of *Finnegans Wake,* and he reviles *Ulysses* as a piece of smut concocted by a collection of "[m]uck-rakers, obscene poets, carnal pimps, sodomous sycophants, pedlars of the colored lusts of fallen humanity" (193). This Joyce is still a writer, though, but he writes only religious documents, "mostly pamphlets for the Catholic Truth Society of Ireland" (192). However, the originality of these compositions is called into question by Joyce himself,

6. Elsewhere, O'Brien indicates that a "capacity for humour" was Joyce's greatest quality, comparing that capacity to Shakespeare's and finding it superior to that of Rabelais ("A Bash in the Tunnel" 208).

further undermining his authorial position: "Writing is not quite the word. Assembly, perhaps, is better—or accretion" (145).[7]

O'Brien's satirical thrust in *The Dalkey Archive* is characteristically dialogic, however. His depiction of Joyce as an ultrapious Catholic contributes to the parodic treatment of religion in the book, but it simultaneously contributes to a similar parody of *attacks* on religion, which are often just as dogmatic and authoritarian as religion itself. Indeed, O'Brien wrote of *The Dalkey Archive* to Timothy O'Keefe that there was "no intention to jeer at God or religion; the idea is to roast the people who seriously do so, and also to chide the Church in certain of its aspects" (cited in Clissmann 294). The ultimate point, with regard to Joyce, seems to be that Joyce's virulent and sustained attack on the church showed that he was in fact much more saturated with Catholicism than he would like to admit.

The attitude toward the church that O'Brien here appears to ascribe to Joyce is quite similar to the one displayed by Stephen Dedalus in *A Portrait of the Artist as a Young Man*. Stephen can consider being a Jesuit priest, or he can consider being a Satanic apostate, but his penchant for idealized visions leaves no room for anything in between. As a result, he remains thoroughly inscribed within the authority of the church, perhaps most so when he is at the height of his rebellion against it. As his friend Cranly perceptively points out to him, "It is a curious thing . . . how your mind is supersaturated with the religion in which you say you disbelieve" (*Portrait* 240).[8]

An almost direct identification of Joyce with Stephen seems to be a consistent element in O'Brien's reading of Joyce. In *The Dalkey Archive*, Mick expresses astonishment that the Joyce he finds appears to bear little relation to Stephen, with the latter's "silence, exile, and cunning" now being replaced by the "garrulous, the repatriate, the ingenuous" (195). This change also signals a submerged critique of Joyce's voluntary exile from the native land where O'Brien chose to remain. Meanwhile, O'Brien continually attacks the aesthetics of stasis and of the God-like artist put forth by Stephen Dedalus in *A Portrait of the Artist as a Young Man*, aesthetics that O'Brien seems to have attributed to Joyce himself.

7. Actually, O'Brien's treatment of Joyce's writing as assembly shows a sophisticated understanding of the real Joyce's composition techniques. Joyce himself once declared (in a letter to George Antheil, January 3, 1931) that he was "quite content to go down to posterity as a scissors and paste man for that seems to me a harsh but not unjust description" (*Letters* 297).

8. Compare O'Brien's suggestion in "A Bash in the Tunnel" that "all true blasphemers must be believers" (202).

Thus, in an interesting way O'Brien seems to have failed to overcome one long-time blind spot in Joyce criticism (the identification of Joyce with Stephen), while at the same time predating even Hugh Kenner in recognizing Stephen's folly and in arguing that Stephen is far from an exemplary model for would-be artists.[9]

Mick contemplates getting Joyce and De Selby together so that they might combine their respective talents in one colossal multidisciplinary creative effort. He imagines the result: "Would Joyce and De Selby combine their staggeringly complicated and diverse minds to produce a monstrous earthquake of a new book, something claiming to supplant the Bible?" (152–53).[10] But this project seems doomed to failure: Joyce's denial of the authorship of *Ulysses* and *Finnegans Wake* and De Selby's questioning of the Bible suggest that the authority of sacred books cannot be trusted. There can be no ultimate book because, as Hackett points out, there is more than one way to tell a story, and even different biblical accounts of the same events are often at odds:

> The Roman Church's Bible has a great lot of material named Apocrypha. There have been apocryphal Gospels according to Peter, Thomas, Barnabas, John, Judas Iscariot and many others. (71)

In any case, O'Brien's fictional Joyce has in mind a far humbler project than writing a replacement Bible—he simply wants to be a Jesuit so that he can work out his abstract theological theories in peace. So Mick gets Joyce in touch with Father Cobble, only to find that the good Father is more concerned with much more mundane things than Joyce's discourse on the *pneuma*. Apparently, the holiest thing about the Jesuits is their underwear, which is all in a state of tatters, and Father Cobble offers Joyce the job of mending them because the Jesuits are not allowed to associate with women, who would normally perform such tasks. The

9. *The Dalkey Archive* was written well after Kenner's demystification of Stephen in works like *Dublin's Joyce*, first published in 1956. But *At Swim-Two-Birds* showed a similar critique of Stephen's aesthetic program as early as 1939. For a discussion of the relationship between *At Swim-Two Birds* and Joyce's *Portrait of the Artist as a Young Man*, see Janik, who notes that "O'Brien saw that Dedalus, viewed from outside, can be rather comic" (67).

10. O'Brien here echoes the suggestion of Northrop Frye that *Finnegans Wake* is of the same genre as the Bible (314). O'Brien also anticipates the argument by Valentine Cunningham that *Finnegans Wake* is, in fact, intended as a replacement for the Bible. But see also my argument elsewhere that *Finnegans Wake* does not present itself as a replacement for the Bible so much as question the authority of "sacred" books in general ("*Finnegans Wake* and *The Satanic Verses*").

combined effect is one last barb at both Joyce and the Jesuits; and Mick leaves guiltily, worrying that he has made a complete fool of Joyce.

Actually, the story of Mick himself provides one of O'Brien's most effective critiques of Joyce—and of mastery. In particular, Mick (like the narrator of *At Swim-Two-Birds*) bears a number of obvious resemblances to Stephen Dedalus. Many of these similarities have to do with the way both characters strive to escape the messiness and contingency of life through a quest for mastery. For Stephen, this quest takes the form first of a turn to religion, then of a turn to art. The drive for dominance that is at the heart of Stephen's project is made clear through Mick's more straightforward depiction of this drive in himself. For example, Mick's illusions of grandeur rival those of Stephen, though without the rhetorical trappings that led a generation of critics to see Stephen as Joyce's depiction of the ideal artist. Midway through *The Dalkey Archive*, Mick begins to take stock of the situation with De Selby and Joyce as he tries to formulate a plan through which he can save not only the world but heaven as well. As he does so, he reminds himself of his own greatness, comparing himself (à la Stephen) to Christ:

> Was he losing sight of the increase and significance of his own personal majesty? . . . But his present situation was that he was on the point of rescuing everybody from obliteration, somewhat as it was claimed that Jesus had redeemed all mankind. Was he not himself a god-figure of some sort? (129)

The true nature of Mick's illusions of power and mastery becomes increasingly clear as he becomes more and more involved in attempting to dominate and manipulate those around him, even when they are great figures like Joyce, De Selby, and even Augustine: "He rather admired his own adroit manipulation of matters which, in certain regards, transcended this world" (151). Mick's project is so grand that he begins to think of himself as a direct emissary of God:

> Mick noted that his own function and standing had risen remarkably. He was *supervising* men of indeterminate calibre, of sanity that was more than suspect. Clearly enough this task had been assigned to him by Almighty God, and this gave him somewhat the status of priest. (156)

Indeed, in a possible parody of Stephen's meditations on entering the priesthood in *Portrait*, Mick begins seriously to consider the possibility of joining the ministry. But in *The Dalkey Archive* such fantasies are clearly antithetical to life in the real world, and so it comes as no surprise that Mick decides that he wants to join some order that will be removed as far as possible from the secular world, perhaps the Cistercians. To do so, he must renounce various vices (like his fondness for drink), and he must also break off his relationship with his girlfriend, Mary, pious though she may be.

Unfortunately, all of Mick's illusions of mastery turn out to be just that. He steals De Selby's supply of D.M.P. and deposits it in the Bank of Ireland, only to find that he has thereby saved the dangerous substance from destruction in a subsequent fire at De Selby's residence.[11] His efforts to recuperate Joyce result only in Joyce's humiliation at the hands of the crude Father Cobble. And his project of escaping from physicality into the ideal spiritual world of the priesthood comes crashing down when he learns that Mary is considering a marriage with Hackett, whereupon Mick becomes jealous and decides to marry her himself. Mary accepts his proposal, and the book ends as she informs him that she is pregnant.

Mick's treatment of Mary provides one of the strongest parallels between himself and Stephen Dedalus. On the one hand, Stephen is attracted by idealized images of purity, as exemplified by the Virgin Mary. He uses such images as objects of imaginary identification that allow him to envision his own freedom from contamination by the physical. On the other, he projects onto real-world women, as exemplified by the Dublin whores, the qualities of physical grossness and disgust which he seeks to expel from his own image. Suzette Henke summarizes this view, noting that to Stephen women "stand as emblems of the flesh—frightening reminders of sex, generation, death" (82). This Augustinian rejection of the physical derives at least partly from Stephen's Catholic upbringing, and it is not insignificant that the hellfire-and-brimstone sermon at the retreat that leads him to repudiate the whores features a standard condemnation of Eve as the temptress who led Adam into sin.

Mick, too, feels that he must repudiate Mary in order to become spiritually pure. As he begins to contemplate joining the priesthood, his attitude toward Mary is increasingly marked by revulsion: "What was she, really, but a gilded trollop, probably with plenty of other gents who were devout associates. Or slaves, marionettes?" (155). Mick's rejection

---

11. In *The Saints Go Cycling In,* Hugh Leonard's stage adaptation of *The Dalkey Archive,* Mick's machinations lead to even more cataclysmic results. He dumps the D.M.P. in the ocean, only to find that seawater is the substance which activates its deadly effects. O'Brien reportedly approved of this darker ending quite heartily.

of Mary is a rejection of life itself, and of all of the physicality and mortality attendant thereto. As Hackett succinctly puts it, "One thing about Mary—she's alive" (220). O'Brien is no feminist, but he frequently shows an awareness of the plight of women in Irish society. Here, he goes to great pains to demonstrate the fatuousness of Mick's attitude toward Mary—and simultaneously to offer a critique of Stephen's attitude toward E—C— and the other women he encounters in *Portrait*. Far from being an unthinking, purely physical being, Mary in fact appears to be more intelligent and articulate than Mick himself:

> Mary was an unusual girl. She was educated, with a year in France, and understood music. She had wit, could be lively, and it took little to induce for a while gaiety of word and mood. . . . She read a lot, talked politics often and once even mentioned her intention of writing a book. (59)

Indeed, it is Mary whom Mick hopes to induce to write the definitive book on Joyce once he can garner the latter's cooperation: "The true story of Joyce would be ideal material for the exercise of her rich mind. She would produce her own unprecedented book" (115).

Mick's later rejection of Mary is thus doubly misguided: first, it is wrong to identify Mary strictly with the physical (regardless of the long tradition behind such stereotypical views of women), and second, it is foolish to attempt to eject the physical from his life in order to gain mastery of his own existence. It is within the discourse of mastery that the motivation behind Mick's equation of Mary with physicality becomes clear: neither Mary as feminine Other nor physicality as inescapable fact of his own existence can be mastered. This point is especially brought home in the ending, when Mick's grandiose plans fall apart as he succumbs to both Mary (in the form of their betrothal) and physicality (in the form of her pregnancy).

The ending of *The Dalkey Archive* appears at first glance to be a rather traditional romantic/comic resolution: man and woman agree to be wed, and then plan for a happy life together ever after. Indeed, Clissmann has emphasized the recuperative possibilities of this ending, arguing that the book "ends with chaos averted and with the resumption of the relationship between Mick and Mary as it had been in the beginning" (322). But the relationship between Mick and Mary, transformed from a relatively casual courtship to a betrothal, is not at all as it was in the beginning. Clissmann sees Mary's pregnancy as a sort of *deus ex machina* resolving all the book's uncertainties, as the "final mystery and, perhaps, the final miracle" (322). But things remain highly uncertain, and the ending is not nearly so neat as it might appear. De Selby is still on the loose, we still don't know what will happen to Joyce, and the D.M.P. substance waits ominously in the vaults of the Bank of Ireland. In fact, the various strands of the plot start to unravel in all directions as the book comes to an end, and the intrusion of Mary into Mick's neat plans actually represents an irruption of chaos within his rage for order rather than the reverse.

We don't even know for sure that Mary is pregnant. Explaining to Mick that it will be nice to have a house for their family, she ends the book by telling him that "I'm certain I'm going to have a baby" (222). It would certainly be possible to interpret this statement simply as a confident prediction that she will be pregnant at some future date, presumably after the marriage. And even if one does conclude that Mary is already pregnant (admittedly the more interesting interpretation), this situation would not be nearly so idyllic as the one Clissmann depicts. For one thing, in Irish society a pregnancy outside of wedlock can hardly be considered unequivocally good news. And despite her suggestive name, Mary's pregnancy can easily be explained without recourse to the miraculous by anyone with even the most rudimentary knowledge of biology. The only question seems to be whether the father is Mick or Hackett because Mary and Hackett have "been going to shows and pubs and dances for weeks and weeks . . . and weeks" and at one point plan to be married (220, O'Brien's ellipsis).

This suggestion of uncertain parentage (another favorite theme of both Joyce and his creation Stephen Dedalus) is the final blow to Mick's pretensions to mastery. The physical reality is that paternity is indeed a legal fiction, and Mick, who had once seen himself as savior and master of earth and heaven, must now come face to face with the fact that he cannot even be sure that he is the father of his "own" child. But such, *The Dalkey Archive* teaches us again and again, is life. Physical reality dictates that a man's reach will inevitably exceed his grasp, and appeals to heaven cannot change that basic fact.

The unraveling of *The Dalkey Archive* in its final pages mirrors the multiple and fragmentary nature of the book as a whole. But, in the tradition of Menippean works like *A Tale of a Tub* and *Tristram Shandy*, this lack of unity itself serves a thematic function. The various languages of science, religion, philosophy, and literature meet and clash in the book, all vying for dominance and all failing to achieve supremacy. The lack of a single master discourse leads to fragmentation but also offers a subversive commentary on mastery in general. The political implications of this conflict of discourses are especially clear when viewed through the optic of Bakhtin's claims that language is always interested, always invested with ideological force, and that any work that seeks to explore the workings of language unavoidably investigates the ideological climate of its world: "In the novel formal markers of languages, manners and styles are symbols for sets of social beliefs" (*Dialogic* 357).

An identification of *The Dalkey Archive* with Bakhtin's comments on the novel and on the tradition of Menippean satire helps to illuminate the way O'Brien's polyphonic book directly demonstrates the impossibility of a completely monologic mastery of language. The book at times seems to get out of hand, so much so that Clissmann—always looking for organic order—is led to conclude that "it is in many ways a sadly confused book, formless and without a single focus" (296). But this lack of focus serves a positive function, contributing to the powerful critique of mastery and monologism that permeates the entire book. O'Brien's extended, career-long critique of Joyce indicates his suspicion of Joyce's mastery of the craft of authorship; and so perhaps it is entirely appropriate that O'Brien faltered in achieving such mastery. This is not to say that O'Brien cleverly and intentionally failed to master his own material in order to make a point. But *The Dalkey Archive* ultimately exceeds any intentions that O'Brien might have had and that the untidiness of this excess in many ways tends to enrich the book as a thoroughgoing critique of mastery in general.

8

Flann O'Brien in the Twentieth Century

Flann O'Brien richly deserves to be included with James Joyce and Samuel Beckett as the three great Irish fiction writers of the twentieth century. And if O'Brien is the least "great" of these three writers, he is also the most Irish. Both Joyce and Beckett tend to be seen as cosmopolitan writers of the world who happen to have been Irish, and their work is widely read within the context of broad international literary trends. O'Brien, on the other hand, has been read almost exclusively within an Irish context. But if O'Brien's work is comparable to that of Joyce and Beckett in many ways, then one would expect that O'Brien's work should resonate with trends that go far beyond the bounds of Irish literature. To conclude my study of O'Brien's fiction, then, I would like to explore some of these resonances in order to place O'Brien's work in a larger context and to illuminate the significance of his writing from some different perspectives. O'Brien was influenced by an international array of writers, he himself influenced a number of writers who came after him, and his work bears resemblances to that of many other writers even when there is probably no direct influence involved.

I have emphasized throughout this book O'Brien's central participation in the tradition of Menippean satire, a participation that already places him in the company not only of Irish writers like Swift and Joyce but of a variety of others, including predecessors like Petronius, Apuleius, Chaucer, Rabelais, Cervantes, and Sterne, and modern successors like Salman Rushdie, Günter Grass, Thomas Pynchon, and Carlos Fuentes.[1] Among other things, reading O'Brien within the context of

1. See Palmeri for an interesting treatment of the continuity of Menippean satire from Petronius through Swift, Gibbon, and Melville on to Pynchon and Borges.

121

Menippean satire helps to emphasize the social and political relevance of his work and to highlight the way his work continues to conduct experimental investigations of language and fiction throughout his career. Even late works like *The Hard Life* and *The Dalkey Archive*—often read as conventional realistic fiction—participate in this experimental project. Most obviously, O'Brien participates in a central way in the rise to prominence of metafiction in the past few decades, a phenomenon that can count writers like Cervantes, Sterne, and Joyce as important models, but for which O'Brien, especially in *At Swim-Two-Birds,* can also be counted as a major modern inspiration. Both in terms of its reflexive concern with its own status as fiction and of its destabilization of traditional ontological boundaries, O'Brien's work resonates with important movements in postmodernist fiction in general. Brian McHale suggests that the most important distinguishing characteristic of postmodernist fiction is its interrogation of the normal ontological boundaries between different levels of existence. Not surprisingly, he includes both *At Swim-Two-Birds* and *The Third Policeman* as central examples of postmodernist fiction. In the same vein, A. A. Mendilow relates *At Swim* to the work of Gide, Huxley, and Pirandello in its "treatment of the planes of reality" (227).

O'Brien was an influential pioneer in many postmodernist techniques. Jerome Klinkowitz notes the important influence of O'Brien's writing on a whole range of experimental American writers in the sixties, including Kurt Vonnegut, Jr., Donald Barthelme, and Ishmael Reed, as well as a number of lesser-known figures (31). Similarly, Sue Asbee catalogs numerous close parallels between B. S. Johnson's metafictional novel *Travelling People* and *At Swim-Two-Birds* (124–26).[2] Perhaps more importantly, Asbee also notes specific references to O'Brien's work in the reflexive fictions of Alasdair Gray (*Lanark*), Anthony Burgess (*Earthly Powers*), John Fowles (*Mantissa*), and Gilbert Sorrentino (*Mulligan Stew*) (126–29).

Sorrentino provides what is probably the most obvious example of O'Brien's influence on the metafictional writers who came after him. *Mulligan Stew* openly acknowledges its debt to *At Swim-Two-Birds,* both through the direct borrowing of characters like Dermot Trellis and Antony and Sheila Lamont and through the book's dedication: "To the memory of Brian O'Nolan—his 'virtue *hilaritas*'." Indeed, *Mulligan Stew* resembles *At Swim-Two-Birds* in numerous ways, having apparently been

---

2. José Lanters anticipates Asbee by noting that Johnson's "theory of fiction in *Travelling People,* published in 1963, shows a remarkable similarity to the theory advocated by the narrator in *At Swim*" (268).

constructed as a "self-evident sham" very much along the lines recommended by O'Brien's novelist narrator. *Mulligan Stew*—as its title indicates—is constructed from a heterogenous mixture of materials from a variety of sources, ranging from the sublime to the ridiculous. Not only its characters, but its very language are obviously borrowed from elsewhere, leading an unidentified voice in a section of the book labeled "An Anonymous Sketch" to launch a vitriolic attack on an unnamed novelist (presumably Lamont, but obviously Sorrentino as well), accusing that novelist of a variety of offenses, including plagiarism:

> Borrowing? Aye! From the base, the sublime, from the low to the high this thief took his ore. Reading a read of a novel he'd pull out a phrase or a line; he ransacked the news; squeezed out the juice from advertisements; was pleased when a song had a word he could use; in the blues he perversely found humor; from Natchez to Mobile he ranged, from the shining mind of heaven to the primordial ooze. A persistent and underground rumor ran thus: that with unparalleled insolence he stole his very characters—all of whom (but of course) were invented by better than he. (261)

This passage describes the method of construction of both *Mulligan Stew* and *At Swim-Two-Birds* quite well. It is especially reminiscent of Niall Sheridan's recollections of O'Brien's activities while composing *At Swim:*

> As the book progressed, Brian gleefully borrowed any material that came to hand. One day, I showed him a sales letter from a Newmarket tipster and it turned up *in toto* in the next wad of typescript that he
> O produced. About the same time, I had done some translations from Catullus and he asked me for a copy of one of these. Later, it came out . . . in *At Swim*. (Sheridan 45)

Indeed, O'Brien's bricolage method in *At Swim* not only anticipates Sorrentino and echoes Joyce but participates in a quite broad trend in modern literature.[3] This method lies very much at the heart of the tradition of Menippean satire, recalling the patchwork texts of authors like Chaucer and Rabelais, as well as those of Menippean postmodernists like Pynchon and Ismael Reed. Also, numerous modern authors have produced texts that in one way or another have been patched together from bits and pieces of other texts, ranging from the broken images of Eliot's *Waste*

---

3. I discuss this and other aspects of Sorrentino's work within the context of writers like Joyce and O'Brien in *Techniques of Subversion* (72–101).

Land to the collage-like constructions of Dos Passos to the parodic documentary technique of the Yugoslavian writer Danilo Kiš to the complex assemblage of quotations from historical texts in the Latin American Eduardo Galeano. Gregory Ulmer goes as far as to suggest that "collage is the single most revolutionary formal innovation in artistic representation to occur in our century" (86). And though collage is not as much a twentieth-century innovation as Ulmer here indicates (he himself admits that it has ancient roots), his point concerning its importance in modern art is well taken.

One of the closest parallels between *Mulligan Stew* and *At Swim-Two-Birds* concerns the way fictional characters sometimes come "unstuck" from their texts, drifting from one ontological level to another. In O'Brien's novel, characters like Shanahan and Lamont revolt against their creator Trellis, while in Sorrentino's novel the character Ned Beaumont escapes from a text being written by Lamont in a protest against Lamont's authorial incompetence. Sorrentino here is obviously working under the direct influence of O'Brien. However, this motif of free-floating characters—which poses some serious ontological questions—occurs quite frequently in modern literature. In addition to Beckett's use of similar devices, one also thinks immediately of the confusion between actors and characters in Luigi Pirandello's *Six Characters in Search of an Author*. One of the modern novels that resembles *At Swim-Two-Birds* most in this respect is Raymond Queneau's *Flight of Icarus*. Queneau's novel includes a character called Morcol, who "has appeared in many novels under different names" (14). Morcol, meanwhile, is a detective who is engaged by the novelist Hubert Lubert to seek the character Icarus, who has disappeared from the manuscript of Lubert's work-in-progress. Morcol, when told of this flight, responds that this development is "extremely Pirandellian" (15), but it is clearly quite O'Brienesque as well. In addition to its focus on the composition of fiction and its confusion of ontological levels, *The Flight of Icarus* features favorite O'Brien motifs like a central emphasis on bicycles.[4] Moreover, as the book's translator notes in her introduction, Queneau is "the master of the intentionally awful pun" (Barbara Wright 5) and his encyclopedic fictions tend to be constructed

4. An important motif in the book has to do with the introduction of bicycles to Paris and the resultant controversy over the exposure of the bloomers of women who ride bicycles. This association of bicycles with the sexual obviously recalls O'Brien, though a more direct referent of the motif would seem to be Joyce's *Ulysses*, in which Gerty Mac-Dowell muses on "unfeminine" girls, "cyclists showing off what they hadn't got" (*Ulysses* 293).

from "an intricate mixture of . . . disparate elements" (7)—both central characteristics of O'Brien's work.[5]

The resemblances between O'Brien's work and that of the American Sorrentino or of the Frenchman Queneau already indicate that O'Brien participates in important literary trends that are international in scope. But the relevance of O'Brien's work within such broad contexts should come as no surprise. For one thing, O'Brien was a sophisticated and well-read writer, his ongoing dialogue with the indigenous folk culture of Ireland notwithstanding. The young Brian O'Nolan read most of the major writers of his time in preparation for his own writing career. Sheridan notes how his friend and college classmate "read everything he could get his hands on," resulting in a mélange of reading material that included the works not only of the Irishmen Joyce, Yeats, and Beckett but also Americans like Dos Passos, Hemingway, and Fitzgerald, and Europeans like Proust and Kafka. Sheridan relates that O'Nolan sometimes railed against "layabouts from slums of Europe poking around in their sickly little psyches," but that O'Nolan admired the works of authors like Proust and Kafka (along with the philosopher Kierkegaard) a great deal (39–40).

The link to Kafka and Kierkegaard provides an especially convenient starting point for examining O'Brien's place in the larger context of twentieth-century literature, because these are two of the few European writers to whom his work has already been compared. Much of O'Brien's work, especially *The Third Policeman*, has an air of absurdity (and of pessimism) that immediately suggests the work of Kafka, as well as the whole modern tradition of existentialism. Francis Doherty compares the world of *The Third Policeman* with the hell of Jean-Paul Sartre's *No Exit* and with the atmosphere often found in plays of the theater of the absurd. Doherty also notes the similar estrangement between language and reality that occurs in *The Third Policeman*, Sartre's *Nausea*, and Beckett's *Watt*. He notes, however, that O'Brien's book does take on a special flavor from its dialogue with the Irish folk tradition, comparing the hell of *The Third Policeman* to *Tir na Nog*, "the idyllic, unchanging other-world of ancient Irish myth, seen in the medieval Irish tales like *The*

5. I know of no direct evidence that Queneau knew O'Brien's work or was influenced by it. The two were roughly contemporaries (Queneau was born in 1903 and died in 1976), but *At Swim* predates *The Flight of Icarus* by nearly three decades. There is a strong Irish connection in Queneau's work, however. For example, Brandon Kershner details the influence of Queneau on Iris Murdoch in his essay "A French Connection." More importantly, Queneau was quite strongly influenced by Joyce, whom he admired greatly. The Queneau-Joyce relationship is elaborated in detail in Kershner's 1972 doctoral dissertation.

Voyage of Bran" (58). Doherty further suggests a kinship with other Irish tales of visits to strange lands like the *Vita Brendasc* (63). In a similar vein, Roy L. Hunt points out some of the echoes of the philosophy of Kierkegaard in O'Brien's explorations of the role of the author but focuses primarily on the implications of O'Brien's retellings of traditional Irish stories from sources like *Buile Suibne* and *Immram Maile Duin*.

The dual emphases of both Doherty and Hunt on O'Brien's similarities to modern continental writers and philosophers and on his dialogue with the Irish cultural tradition point toward what may perhaps be the most important feature of O'Brien's work—his ability to address many of the same issues and concerns as his contemporaries from around the world while recasting these issues and concerns in a distinctively Irish mold. Such combinations of the general and the specific are a hallmark of Joyce's writing as well, and the resulting intercultural dialogues suggest, among other things, that many of the social, cultural, and political problems of Ireland parallel those in a number of other modern cultures—a conclusion that helps to explain how Irish writers have been able to attain such a central place in modern literary history. For example, if by writing in English Irish writers like O'Brien and Joyce are writing in the language of a foreign power, then they are very much in the same position as a Central European like Franz Kafka, a Jew in Prague writing in the German of an Austro-Hungarian Empire from which Czechoslovakia emerged as an independent state only late in Kafka's short life.

There are numerous parallels between the situation of Ireland under the British Empire (and its aftermath) and that of much of Central Europe under Austro-Hungarian Empire rule.[6] These parallels were widely recognized in Ireland itself, and it is no accident that Leopold Bloom—perhaps the most important character in all of Joyce's work—is of Hungarian ancestry. Andras Ungar discusses the way Bloom's origins are at least partly a reference to the suggestion by the Irish nationalist leader Arthur Griffith that Ireland should look to Hungary's success in gaining autonomy under the Hapsburgs as a model for their own struggles

6. Many aspects of O'Brien's work recall that of Central and Eastern European writers. The Czech Jaroslav Hašek's *Good Soldier Svejk* contains numerous Menippean elements in its satirization of the Austro-Hungarian Empire in World War I. The Polish writer Witold Gombrowicz also employs numerous Menippean and grotesque elements in his work, while Gombrowicz's countryman Bruno Schulz makes important use of myth and the fantastic. The Czech modernist Karel Čapek parallels O'Brien in his emphasis on satire and use of the fantastic. And the contemporary Czech writer Milan Kundera produces metafictional works that are constructed as polyphonic patchworks of competing discourses.

against English domination.[7] In particular, Ungar notes that Joyce (who himself lived under Hapsburg rule for years in Trieste) rejected Griffith's analogy as unrealistic; Ungar thus sees Joyce's reinscription of the motif as parodic. Indeed, the realities of Irish politics made the analogy with Hungary meaningful at best in a metaphorical sense, not as a basis for the kind of concrete political action that Griffith and his allies sought. But Bloom's Hungarian origins do contribute in an important way to his alienation from the society around him, as does the Jewish element of his heritage. Most of O'Brien's characters fit more naturally into Irish society than does Bloom, but the kind of estrangement experienced by Bloom in Dublin is very reminiscent of the situation of the unnamed narrator in *The Third Policeman,* or even of Bonaparte O'Coonassa. It is also quite reminiscent of the alienation of Kafka characters like Joseph K. in *The Trial* and K. in *The Castle,* with both the Central European and the Jewish elements of Bloom's background suggesting Kafka as well.

O'Brien's work bears many similarities to that of Kafka, though these similarities have received surprisingly little critical attention. For example, Anne Clissmann's book—the richest available compendium of sheer information about O'Brien and his writing—does not mention Kafka at all. Kafka's work has been seen by many as a paradigmatic expression of the fundamental predicament of modern man. A comparison with Kafka thus promises to do a great deal to illuminate the significance of O'Brien's work within the context of modernity. There are mythical and spiritual echoes in the works of both writers, but these echoes sound in harmony with very down-to-earth motifs like satires of bumbling and inefficient bureaucracies. For example, the ordeal of Joseph K. in Kafka's *Trial* is no doubt usefully read as an allegory of the universal alienation and guilt of humanity in a fallen world—but it is at the same time very much a commentary on the immense bureaucratic apparatus of the Austro-Hungarian Empire and its aftermath. Similarly, the trial of Dermot Trellis in *At Swim-Two-Birds* has universal and mythical resonances, even as it also suggests a mockery of the legal system in Ireland.

Both Kafka and O'Brien feature a number of grotesque elements in their works, a tendency that frequently leads to a mood of comedy interlaced with terror. The most obviously Kafkaesque of O'Brien's writings is *The Third Policeman,* in which the depiction of absurd legal proceedings again recalls *The Trial,* but in which the overall tone and contents

7. Joyce himself points to this link directly in *Ulysses.* One of the many far-fetched rumors about Bloom that float about in Dublin is that Bloom himself was a major inspiration behind Griffith's ideas: "Bloom gave the ideas for Sinn Fein to Griffith to put in his paper" (275).

are especially reminiscent of *The Castle*. In both texts an anonymous (or semi-anonymous) hero wanders fruitlessly in search of a goal that is not only unreachable but largely undefined. Kafka's K. spends the entire text of *The Castle* trying to make contact with the mysterious Castle authorities, though the ultimate purpose of this contact is not at all clear. The unnamed narrator of *The Third Policeman*, meanwhile, spends most of that book trying "[t]o find what I am looking for" (48), though just what this might be is again open to question. Both of these impossible quests are highly epistemological in nature. As Heinz Politzer suggests, the futility of K.'s efforts in *The Castle* shows that "attempts to penetrate the mystery of the world are bound to end in ultimate failure" (42), a conclusion that might equally well be applied to *The Third Policeman*.

But the various parallels between *The Castle* and *The Third Policeman* go far beyond such general resemblances, offering significant possibilities for an intertextual dialogue that enriches the reading of both texts. O'Brien suggests the futility of human epistemological inquiry largely through a down-to-earth parody of the excesses of scholarly research, with larger, more religious resonances sounding in the margins to suggest that there are simply things in the world that exceed the bounds of human understanding. In *The Castle*, however, Kafka seems to reverse this emphasis—the primary focus is on the Castle as an emblem of other-worldly mystery, with a secondary parody of bureaucratic complexity and obfuscation as a roadblock to genuine understanding in the secular world. As a result, *The Castle* helps to highlight the mystical elements of *The Third Policeman*, while *The Third Policeman* reinforces the political satire of *The Castle*. Reading the two texts together, then, enriches the dialogue between the mystical and the mundane, the universal and the particular that already informs both novels.

This kind of dialogue is very central to the so-called mythic method, in which very particular contemporary events and characters (like Dermot Trellis and his torture at the hands of his rebellious characters) are placed in dialogic opposition to more universal, mythic figures (like King Sweeney and his suffering, which serves as a clear prototype for Irish experience as a whole). O'Brien's use of the mythic method most obviously suggests a comparison with Joyce, of course, but Kafka uses the technique as well. In a crucial scene in *The Castle*, K. finally makes contact with a Castle official, the secretary Bürgel. But, as Bürgel relates potentially crucial information about the workings of the Castle bureaucracy, K. nods off to sleep and dreams of himself doing battle with a "secretary, naked, very like the statue of a Greek god" (342). But when he awakes, he is jolted back to reality at the sight of Bürgel's bare chest:

"Here you have your Greek god!" (343). The disjunction between the bureaucrat Bürgel and the Greek god is highly reminiscent of that between Joyce's Leopold Bloom and Homer's Ulysses or that between the modern Dublin and the mythic Irish past in O'Brien's *At Swim-Two-Birds*. Indeed, when Politzer describes the effect of "the heroic mingling with the trivial" in this mythic method as "an absurd tragicomedy that seems to be mocking itself" (40–41) he captures an important element of the work of Joyce and O'Brien, as well as Kafka.

The conflation of the mythic and the mundane in K.'s encounter with Bürgel centrally informs every element of *The Castle*. Kafka's Castle looms above a village over which it has authority, but with which its communication is only of the most strained and indirect kind. The officials of the Castle are extremely nebulous figures, respected and feared by the inhabitants of the village, but hardly understood by them. Central among these figures is the elusive Klamm, the dignitary with whom K. spends most of the book trying (unsuccessfully) to gain an audience. And Klamm is an enigmatic figure indeed, as Olga explains to K. during a pivotal conversation:

> Some people have seen him, everybody has heard of him, and out of glimpses and rumors and through various distorting factors an image of Klamm has been constructed which is certainly true in fundamentals. But only in fundamentals. In detail it fluctuates, and yet perhaps not so much as Klamm's real appearance. For he's reported as having one appearance when he comes into the village and another on leaving it, after having his beer he looks different from what he does before it, when he's awake he's different from when he's asleep, when he's alone he's different from when he's talking to people, and—what is comprehensible after all that—he's almost another person up in the Castle. (231)

The religious aura surrounding Klamm in the text is quite obvious, and he can even be seen as a figure of God. He is a very similar figure to the shifting and changing Mr. Knott of Beckett's *Watt* (who carries some of the same religious resonances), but he is also quite reminiscent of Policeman Fox, the elusive "third policeman" of O'Brien's title.[8] Thus, when O'Brien's narrator first arrives at the book's strange police station he

---

8. Ruby Cohn presents an extended discussion of the similarities (and differences) between *The Castle* and *Watt*, including a comparison of Klamm and Knott. Meanwhile, Doherty suggests numerous similarities between *Watt* and *The Third Policeman*. The two essays together thus point toward certain parallels between *The Third Policeman* and *The Castle*.

meets Sergeant Pluck and Policeman MacCruiskeen but learns from Pluck that Fox is not so easy to track down:

> we never see him or hear tell of him at all because he is always on his beat and never off it and he signs the book in the middle of the night when even a badger is asleep. He is mad as a hare, he never interrogates the public and he is always taking notes. (77)

Fox—like Klamm and Knott—is a sort of God-like figure, but he is first and foremost a burly Irish policeman of the sort that O'Brien (and Beckett) so loved to lampoon. Indeed, Fox, master of the substance omnium, is virtually all-powerful, but his imagination is so prosaic that he can think of only the most mundane of miracles to perform. Omnium makes all things possible, but for Fox it is especially useful for "taking the muck off your leggings in winter" (189) and as "a great convenience for boiling eggs" (190). The disjunction between Fox's exotic powers and his vapid mind makes for some good comedy, but it also emphasizes the mixture of the sacred and the secular that so importantly informs O'Brien's book. Most importantly, that Fox should wield such power while being so obviously unqualified to do so in a judicious manner constitutes a fierce condemnation of the secular authorities in Ireland while at the same time suggesting an excessive interest in worldly affairs on the part of the Catholic Church, Ireland's principal spiritual authority.

The obvious political intonation of *The Third Policeman* resonates with a clear element of political satire that resides in *The Castle* as well. The authoritarian symbolism often associated with the police in O'Brien suggests a similar element in Kafka and recalls Theodor Adorno's argument that Kafka's work cites "National Socialism far more than the hidden dominion of God" (259). But if Adorno sees the officials of Kafka's Castle as an uncanny prefiguration of the SS of Hitler and Goebbels, when read with O'Brien, Kafka's Castle irresistibly recalls Dublin Castle, traditional seat of British imperial authority in Dublin. Kafka's book thus becomes not only a commentary on the incommensurability of the physical and spiritual in the modern world but also a satirical depiction of the absurdity of imperialism. Prague in the days of the Austro-Hungarian Empire was as much a colonial city as British Dublin. One recalls here the recognition by Mr. Collopy in *The Hard Life* that he will be unable to communicate his grievances concerning the mistreatment of women in Dublin to the officials of Dublin Castle. Indeed, one of the distinctive features of imperialism in general is the distance and lack of communication between the colonizers and the colonized, a separation that makes each group appear unreal and inhuman to the other, contributing very directly to the kinds of feelings of absurdity that so strongly inform both *The Castle* and *The Third Policeman*.[9] Jeremy Hawthorn describes the effect well in relation to Joseph Conrad's *Heart of Darkness:* "Imperialism is centrally involved in the dream-existence of people in *Heart of Darkness*, for it involves yet more extended, complex and concealed chains of mediation through signs than even life in the domestic city" (22).

Heart of Darkness, itself based on a quest for epistemological closure that remains unsolved, bears numerous resemblances to both *The Castle* and *The Third Policeman*. For example, Conrad's Kurtz clearly belongs to the same family of elusive characters as O'Brien's Fox and Kafka's Klamm, as well as Beckett's Knott. And the overt implication of imperialism in Conrad's text strongly reinforces the more veiled suggestion of imperialism in both *The Castle* and *The Third Policeman*. One of the distinctive features of *Heart of Darkness* is the way it "reveals the collusion of imperialism and patriarchy" (Smith 180), especially in the treatment of Kurtz's "Intended" late in the book. O'Brien's work can be seen to do much the same, especially as O'Brien's treatment of gender issues takes on a considerably more serious intonation when compared with Kafka's more chilling depiction of the plight of women in patriarchal society. In *The Castle* it is clear that K. regards (without a hint of remorse) the barmaid Frieda merely as an instrument for getting to Klamm, and the entire family of the proto-feminist Amalia is ostracized when she refuses the vulgar advances of the Castle official Sortini. Adorno thus notes that in Kafka's work "patriarchal society reveals its true secret, that of direct, barbaric oppression. Women are reified as mere means to an end: as sexual objects and as connections" (263). Women characters in O'Brien like Teresa of *At Swim-Two-Birds*, Annie of *The Hard Life*, and Mary of *The Dalkey Archive* are often objectified as well. Reading Kafka through O'Brien suggests imperialism as a referent of *The Castle*, while reading O'Brien through Kafka brings more sharply into focus O'Brien's criticism of the treatment of women in Irish society. And this dual movement suggests, especially when reinforced with a dash of Conrad, strong similarities between the ideology of imperialism and that of patriarchy. Both imperialism and patriarchy are based on domination of one group by another, a domination that makes true intersubjective communication impossible. It is not insignificant, then, that the difficulty of communication is a central informing characteristic of the absurd worlds depicted by both O'Brien and Kafka.

The characters of O'Brien and Kafka tend to have a great deal of

9. One might also recall here the separation between the Gaels and the Gaeligores of *The Poor Mouth*.

difficulty either in making themselves understood or in understanding others. This difficulty is also experienced by Conrad's Marlow, who suggests first that most of his impressions of Kurtz were derived from vague sensations arising from hearsay and second that it is impossible for him to convey these sensations to his audience, just as it is impossible fully to explain a dream:

> It seems to me I am trying to tell you a dream—making a vain attempt, because no relation of a dream can convey the dream-sensation . . . . No, it is impossible; it is impossible to convey the life-sensation of any given epoch of one's existence—that which makes its truth, its meaning—its subtle and penetrating essence. It is impossible. We live, as we dream—alone. (95)

Noting this difficulty in communication, Hawthorn suggests that "Marlow, unable to express the 'inexpressible', is able to express its inexpressibility" (28)—which certainly sounds reminiscent of the project of authors like Kafka and Beckett. It is appropriate also to include O'Brien in this group of writers who explore the fundamental limitations of language. *Heart of Darkness, The Castle, Watt,* and *The Third Policeman* all contain numerous instances of problematic communication and interpretation, but in each case the ultimate example of hermeneutic confusion is the text itself. I have discussed elsewhere this motif in both Conrad and Beckett.[10] In the case of Kafka, this motif is rather obvious, permeating the very fabric of his language, which continually teases the reader with its seeming precision and objectivity while at the same time deftly refusing to yield meaning in any simple way. As Adorno suggests, "Each sentence says 'interpret me', and none will permit it" (246).

Kafka reinforces the slippery quality of his individual sentences by embedding in his texts a number of allegories of reading and writing. One thinks, for example, of the horrific writing/execution machine in "In the Penal Colony." In *The Castle* K. encounters unreadable signs virtually everywhere he turns, the most overt of which are probably the two enigmatic letters he receives from Klamm. As Olga explains to K., it is impossible finally to decipher the significance of those letters because "they themselves change in value perpetually, the reflections they give rise to are endless, and chance determines where one stops reflecting, and so even our estimate of them is a matter of chance" (297). These letters are clearly emblems of Kafka's text itself, much in the way that the letter of Biddy the Hen represents an interior duplication of the entire text of

---

10. On *Heart of Darkness,* see my "Horror of Mortality." On *Watt,* see *Literature and Domination.*

Finnegans Wake. And the endless hermeneutic chains triggered by these letters are reminiscent not only of the *Wake* but of the infinite regressions embedded in O'Brien texts like *At Swim-Two-Birds* and *The Third Policeman*.

As I have argued throughout this book, O'Brien maintains a focus on language (and particularly the inability of language adequately to convey experience in the modern world) throughout his career. Including O'Brien in the company of writers like Kafka and Beckett, who similarly explore the failure of language, does a great deal to illuminate his place in twentieth-century literature. The usual perception of O'Brien's career is that he begins in an experimental modernist mode but gradually drifts toward the use of more and more conventional language as his career proceeds. For example, Ian MacKenzie suggests that O'Brien "seems to be the only writer to have begun his career as a modernist and then reverted to a kind of naturalism" (55). On the other hand, even Mac-Kenzie acknowledges that O'Brien to some extent continued to distance himself from ordinary uses of language throughout his career and that O'Brien's last three "realist" novels have plots "no realist would contemplate" (60). Reading O'Brien through Kafka, one might even suggest that O'Brien's movement was not from modernism to naturalism as much as from the kind of modernism represented by Joyce to the kind represented by Kafka. Kafka, after all, writes crisp, clear, declarative sentences that seem a far cry from the opaque constructions associated with Joycean modernism, yet Kafka makes a profound statement about the unbridgeable gap between language and reality in the way that his seemingly straightforward writing still refuses to yield anything like definitive interpretations.[11] O'Brien's increasingly "pedestrian" language may not represent a reversion to naturalism so much as a movement beyond his initial modernism owing to a growing recognition that the modernist project of linguistic revolution was doomed to failure. Writers like Joyce might seek to defamiliarize language itself in an attempt to shatter habitual modes of perception and thereby to gain new insights into reality, but writers like Kafka, Beckett, and O'Brien seem to feel that no amount of intentional defamiliarization can reduce the essential foreignness of a world that, as Wallace Stevens put it, "is not our own."

Much of the air of doubleness and duplicity that informs all of O'Brien's work can be seen to arise from his paradoxical perception that the modern world is both hopelessly banal and irreducibly strange. Thus,

---

11. By "Joycean" modernism I mean the kind of overt linguistic experimentation usually associated with Joyce. Joyce, himself, however, was probably closer to Kafka and Beckett in his realization of the limitations of language than is usually acknowledged.

when O'Brien combines depiction of the sterile squalor of everyday life in Dublin with highly imaginative fantasy, he achieves the dual effect of suggesting alternatives to the quotidian even as he simultaneously suggests the banality of many products of the imagination. O'Brien's deadpan mixture of the fantastic and the ordinary again places him in the midst of important trends in modern literary history. For example, his work resonates in some obvious ways with the technique of "magic realism" popularized by Latin American writers like Gabriel García Márquez and also used extensively by such writers as Rushdie, who openly acknowledges O'Brien as a predecessor. And if the leap from Kafka to García Márquez seems a large one, perhaps the size of that step further emphasizes the breadth of O'Brien's relevance to modern literature. On the other hand, García Márquez himself was strongly influenced by Kafka, and the fictional worlds of his novels often have a somewhat Kafkaesque quality, just as certain oppressive realities of life in Latin America mirror those in Eastern Europe.[12]

Ireland shares many of these realities as well, and a work like García Márquez's *One Hundred Years of Solitude* recalls O'Brien in numerous ways. In addition to its destabilization of the boundary between reality and fantasy, *One Hundred Years* uses indigenous folk culture as an important source of material, carries on a specific dialogue with imperialism, and draws on a wide range of other texts, literary or otherwise. Moreover, the climax of the book involves a moment of self-referential ontological instability of the kind so central to *At Swim-Two-Birds*. In this climax the last in a long line of Aureliano Buendías finally deciphers the manuscripts left by the gypsy Melquíades, only to reveal that this manuscript is the text of *One Hundred Years* itself. And this discovery leads to the apocalyptic end of the text, an ending that recalls that of *The Dalkey Archive*, especially as it resonates with hints throughout García Márquez's text of the apocalyptic potential of science.[13]

The implied critique of science in García Márquez works like *One Hundred Years of Solitude* and *Love in the Time of Cholera* (as well as in O'Brien texts like *The Third Policeman* and *The Dalkey Archive*) participates in the dialogue between the magical and the mundane that informs

12. García Márquez was also influenced by other leading modernists like Joyce, Woolf, and Faulkner, in addition to Kafka. See Levitt. On parallels between Latin America and Eastern Europe, see Fuentes.

13. Brian Conniff notes that *One Hundred Years* shows magic realism to have a dark side. For Conniff this technique cannot only depict magical ways of transcending the confusion of modern life but can also depict the apocalypse (168). Moreover, "[a]pocalypse is only the logical consequence of imperialist oppression, supported by science" (178).

magic realism in general. And this opposition can be seen as a variation of a number of other oppositions in modern thought, like the conflict between the Dionysian and the Apollonian that Nietzsche sees as central to ancient Greek drama and that many observers have argued to be an important source of energy in modernism.[14] Forms of this dialogue— variously figured as an opposition between passion and abstraction, the irrational and the rational, poetry and science, and so forth—can be found in the work of any number of modern writers.

Shifting back to Eastern Europe, this duality is especially central to modern Russian literature, and reading O'Brien within that context offers an additional perspective on the relevance of his work to general movements in modern culture.[15] Russian culture may be distinguished by its relative isolation from trends in the remainder of Europe, but connections do remain, and the great nineteenth-century Russian novelists were highly influential in the West.[16] O'Brien's work resonates with that of Russian writers in a number of ways. For example, the Russian emigré Vladimir Nabokov joins O'Brien as an important inspiration for metafictional writers of the past three decades. Nabokov satires like *Pale Fire* have much in common with O'Brien's work, and Nabokov's early *Invitation to a Beheading* parallels *The Third Policeman* in numerous ways. In addition, early-twentieth-century writers like Yury Olesha, Viktor Shklovsky, Boris Pilnyak, and Yevgeny Zamyatin made extensive use of techniques of textual assemblage similar to those employed by O'Brien.[17] Meanwhile, Bakhtin's great Menippean exemplar Dostoyevski can be seen as the forerunner of a strain that runs throughout modern Russian literature, in which madness, the irrational, and the fantastic are subversively opposed to sanity, reason, and the ordinary, the latter being associated consistently with oppression, political or otherwise.[18]

14. For an extended discussion of this topic, see Spears.

15. The strong tradition of fantastic realism in Russian literature—featuring the work of writers like Gogol, Dostoevsky, and Zamyatin—also bears many similarities to Latin American magical realism.

16. Joyce, for example, was importantly influenced by Russian writers like Dostoevsky, as well as by the nineteenth-century Russian anarchist Mikhail Bakunin. A surprising number of the discussions with Joyce recalled by Arthur Power have to do with Russian literature. For example, Power quotes Joyce as calling Dostoevsky "the man more than any other who has created modern prose, and intensified it to its present-day pitch" (58). See my discussion of Joyce and Bakunin in *Joyce, Bakhtin, and the Literary Tradition*.

17. See Peppard for a discussion of this trend in modern Russian literature, especially in works of Olesha like *Three Fat Men* and *Envy*.

18. Oppressive conditions in Russia have much in common with those in Ireland, even if the former tend to be more overt. For example, in his book *A Tomb for Boris*

This strain in Russian literature has much in common with O'Brien's work.[19] One of the classics in this vein is Mikhail Bulgakov's *Master and Margarita*, a work that recalls much in O'Brien works like *At Swim-Two-Birds*, *The Third Policeman*, and *The Dalkey Archive*. In Bulgakov's book a mysterious sorceror named Woland (Satan) visits modern Moscow with his entourage and wreaks havoc on the populace to punish them for various philistine shortcomings like greed and vanity.[20] Interspersed with the narrative of these modern occurrences are excerpts from a novel about Pontius Pilate written by the "Master" of the title. Bulgakov thus creates a dialogue between events surrounding Woland's visit to Moscow and those surrounding the arrest and crucifixion of one Jeshua (Christ) in ancient Jerusalem. Many general aspects of *The Master and Margarita* thus recall the work of O'Brien: the dual focus on modern social satire and the reinscription of ancient myths, the important use of fantastic and grotesque elements, the use of inserted manuscript fragments, the use of an unnamed writer as a central character. Further, the implication of characters like Woland is highly ambiguous, as this Satanic figure seems morally superior to virtually all of the citizens he encounters in Moscow. This ambiguity recalls the sometimes surprising reversals that occur in O'Brien motifs like the encounter between the Pooka McPhellimey and the Good Fairy in *At Swim-Two-Birds*. Indeed, O'Brien's various dialogues between the flesh and the spirit are highly reminiscent of Bulgakov's work. As Colin Wright suggests, the most general concern of *The Master and Margarita* is with "the conflict of the spiritual with the material world of everyday—a theme that, in one form or another, underlies the whole of Bulgakov" (261).

These general similarities can largely be encompassed within the kind of family resemblances typically associated with works of the same genre, and it is significant that the genre of *The Master and Margarita* has gener-

---

Davidovich, the Yugoslavian writer Danilo Kis suggests strong parallels between the techniques of domination practiced in Stalinist Russia and those traditionally exercised by the Catholic Church. Importantly, one of the major characters in *A Tomb* is an Irishman, and Kis uses Joyce as an important intertextual source. On Kis and Joyce, see the essay by Dubravka Juraga and me.

19. O'Brien mentions the Soviet Union at least once in his work. In his "editor's" foreword to *The Poor Mouth*, he sardonically indicates the difficulty of life in rural Ireland by noting that "emigration is thinning out the remote areas, the young folk are setting their faces towards Siberia in the hope of better weather and relief from the cold and tempest which is natural to them" (9).

20. Bulgakov's book is importantly influenced by Goethe's *Faust*, a work that also figures in O'Brien's career. For example, De Selby is a sort of Faustian figure. Moreover, one of O'Brien's plays, *Faustus Kelly* (featuring an Irish politician who sells his soul to the devil), combines the Faust theme with political satire, as does Bulgakov.

ally been identified as Menippean satire. Edwards, for example, notes that Bulgakov's book includes all fourteen elements associated with the Menippean satire by Bakhtin in *Problems of Dostoevsky's Poetics* (Edwards 147). There are, however, additional specific parallels between Bulgakov and O'Brien that illustrate their common problems and concerns as writers. For example, late in *The Master and Margarita* Woland takes the Master and his inamorata Margarita away from Moscow on a sort of journey into the afterlife, though the Master and Margarita are uncertain during this journey whether they are dead or not. On the trip they observe Pilate (not only a historical personage, but a character in the Master's novel) endlessly agonizing over his complicity in the death of Jeshua, and by the end of the book Bulgakov's novel merges with that of the Master. Meanwhile, the ontological instability brought about by such convergences is further complicated by the fact that both of the book's two major plot lines are intermixed with the dreams of another character, the poet Ivan Homeless.[21] Indeed, some critics feel that the entire text of *The Master and Margarita* is best recuperated as the dream of Ivan. These confusions of ontological levels are quite similar to those that occur in O'Brien texts like *At Swim-Two-Birds*, *The Third Policeman*, and *The Dalkey Archive*, the effect in both authors being to suggest that the reality of life in their respective societies has become so absurd as to be indistinguishable from fiction or dreams.

An important motif in Bulgakov's book concerns the tribulations undergone by the Master at the hands of the literary establishment in response to his novel. In particular, the Master is roundly attacked by critics who accuse him of being, among other things, an apologist for Christianity, and the intensity of these attacks is so severe that the Master burns his manuscript in a fit of despondency. These events rather obviously indicate the difficulties of writers in Stalinist Russia, difficulties that have now been well chronicled in places like Alexander Solzhenitsyn's famous 1967 letter to the Congress of Soviet Writers or in Ilya Ehrenburg's novel *The Thaw*, detailing the despair of authors forced to write in accordance with official doctrine in Stalin's regime. Bulgakov himself suffered such difficulties, and his continued existence in Russia under Stalin was uneasy at best. Indeed, there was little chance that a book like *The Master and Margarita* could be published in Stalinist Russia, though Bulgakov diligently worked on it for over a decade up until his death in 1940.

In *The Master and Magarita* Woland restores the Master's destroyed

21. Ivan's "homelessness" obviously echoes the alienation of characters like Kafka's K. or the narrator of *The Third Policeman*.

manuscript to him, announcing that "manuscripts don't burn" (300). We learn later that the book was really preserved all along, because the Master remembers every word, even without the manuscript (376). And this little allegory of the endurance of writing in the face of oppression and stupidity turns out to be prescient—Bulgakov's own book was finally published more than twenty-five years after his death. The fate of *The Master and Margarita* parallels that of *The Third Policeman* quite closely, just as the burning of the Master's manuscript within Bulgakov's book irresistibly recalls the burning of Dermot Trellis's manuscript in *At Swim-Two-Birds*. The descriptions of these two burnings are almost startlingly similar, both perhaps arising from personal experience, as there could be no possibility of influence by either writer upon the other. When the maid Teresa burns Trellis's book, we are told of the pages that

> now they were blazing, curling and twisting and turning black, straining uneasily in the draught and then taking flight as if to heaven through the chimney, a flight of light things red-flecked and wrinkled hurrying to the sky. (313)

And the Master supplies a parallel description of his burning of his own manuscript:

> This is very difficult to do; paper covered with writing burns very reluctantly. Breaking my nails, I tore the copybooks and slipped the sheets vertically between the logs. I ruffled and beat them with the poker. At times the ashes almost choked the flame, but I fought them, and the novel was dying despite its stubborn resistance. Familiar words flickered before me, the yellow color crept up the pages, but the words stood out on them. They disappeared only when the paper turned black, and furiously I finished them off with the poker. (163–4)

O'Brien's difficulties in publishing *The Third Policeman* were different from those encountered by Bulgakov in Stalinist Russia, but a certain amount of censorship has long been a fact of life in Ireland as well. O'Brien remained embroiled in a number of legal battles throughout most of his career and was highly sensitive to certain limitations on literary freedom in Ireland. For example, he seems to have been convinced that *The Hard Life* would be banned in Ireland.[22] It was not, but in any case O'Brien carried on a running feud with the literary establishment

22. Clissmann documents O'Brien's expectations that *The Hard Life* would be banned, though she suggests that he may even have been disappointed when the book was not suppressed, denying him free publicity (269–71).

throughout his career, and he seems to have shared Bulgakov's sense that the literary powers-that-be were largely composed of unthinking philistines who were unable to appreciate his work. That a book like *The Hard Life* was actually a great success in Ireland, while a somewhat similar Bulgakov satire like *The Heart of a Dog* was never published in Stalinist Russia, indicates the more overt nature of the oppression encountered by Bulgakov relative to that experienced by O'Brien. But in some ways it is the very difference in the political and cultural climates of Bulgakov and O'Brien that makes many of their similarities more striking.

Like his character Bonaparte O'Coonassa, O'Brien's literary reputation has suffered a certain amount of "Gaelic hardship," including "distress, need, ill-treatment, adversity, calamity, foul play, misery, famine and ill-luck" (*Poor* 125). But this quick survey shows that O'Brien's work in fact resembles that of many important modern authors, ranging from Kafka to Conrad to García Márquez to Bulgakov. And these similarities illustrate only a few of the ways in which O'Brien's work participates in broad international trends in modern literary history. Moreover, important themes in his work also resonate with developments in numerous extraliterary fields like science and philosophy. A recognition of O'Brien's engagement with the kinds of issues that have concerned so many other modern thinkers in so many fields from around the world suggests that O'Brien deserves an important place in our figurations of modern literary and intellectual history.

Appendix
Works Cited
Index

Appendix

Flann O'Brien and Bakhtin's
Characteristics of Menippean Satire

In *Problems of Dostoevsky's Poetics* Bakhtin provides a checklist of the fourteen basic features of the Menippean satire (which he often refers to as the "menippea"). This checklist provides a convenient means of comparing specific works of literature to Bakhtin's conception of Menippean satire. I provide in this appendix a brief discussion of O'Brien's work within the context of this checklist in order both to demonstrate how well O'Brien's work matches Bakhtin's list and to provide an introduction to the characteristics of Menippean satire in general. Each of Bakhtin's fourteen characteristics is listed below (with page numbers from *Problems* where appropriate), followed by a brief discussion of how O'Brien's various works display each characteristic.

1. The comic element of the Menippean satire is generally quite important. Moreover, this comedy is generally of a specifically carnivalesque nature.

All of O'Brien's major works are overtly comic in tone, and so the importance of the comic element in his work is entirely obvious. Moreover, O'Brien's comedy is frequently informed by carnivalesque energies. Bakhtin discusses the carnival and the carnivalization of literature in detail in pages 122–37 of *Problems of Dostoevsky's Poetics*. For example, he notes that a primary characteristic of the carnival is its dynamic opposition to the everyday "noncarnival" world. The carnival has a strongly parodic function: it has little meaning alone, but becomes significant only when related to the concepts and forms that it parodies. Thus, one of Bakhtin's favorite examples of carnivalized literature is the ancient Greek satyr play or "fourth drama," a "parodic-travestying" farce that was performed after the typical Greek tragic trilogy, forming an *"indispensible* conclusion to the tragic trilogy" (*Dialogic* 55, Bakhtin's emphasis).

For Bakhtin, an important aspect of these carnivalized parodic exchanges involves the device of "parodying doubles." "They find especially vivid expression in Dostoevsky—almost every one of the leading heroes of his novels has several doubles who parody him in various ways" (127–28). Such doublings also occur prominently in O'Brien, as in the proliferation of author figures in *At Swim-Two-Birds*. Voelker discusses the way in which "[t]winships abound in *The Third Policeman*" (89), Bonaparte O'Coonassa becomes a double of his father in *The Poor Mouth*, and so on.

Elements of parody are of critical importance in O'Brien's work. He frequently parodies particular authors (such as his dialogue with Joyce in works like *At Swim-Two-Birds* or *The Dalkey Archive*). In addition, he often addresses his parodies to specific discourses, especially discourses of authority like science, philosophy, and religion. One thinks here of O'Brien's depictions of the mad scientist-philosopher de Selby (or De Selby), as well as his comic accounts of the shenanigans of de Selby scholars in *The Third Policeman* and his presentation of comic priests like Father Fahrt of *The Hard Life* or Father Cobble of *The Dalkey Archive*. Bakhtin emphasizes that such carnivalesque subversions of authoritarian discourses in the Menippean satire are not pure mockery, but open serious dialogues. Thus, carnivalized literature is inherently "serio-comic" in nature. O'Brien's work is certainly that, often mixing its comedy with serious, even somber elements and intonations.

2. *The Menippean satire generally ignores the bonds of verisimilitude, and is indeed characterized by "an extraordinary freedom of plot and philosophical invention," and by a use of the fantastic. "The fact that the leading heroes of the menippea are historical or legendary figures . . . presents no obstacles" (144).*

Elements of the fantastic are again present in all of O'Brien's works. In *At Swim-Two-Birds*, *The Third Policeman*, and *The Dalkey Archive*, in fact, fantastic situations and occurrences are of obvious and central importance. Even O'Brien's more ostensibly down-to-earth works contain such elements. One need only recall here the "gravid water" supplied by Manus that leads to Collopy's death in *The Hard Life* or the mythical "Sea-cat" that pursues Bonaparte O'Coonassa in *The Poor Mouth*. Numerous historical and legendary personages appear as characters in O'Brien's work, ranging from Irish mythical figures like Finn MacCool and the mad king Sweeney to important figures from Western culture like St. Augustine and James Joyce. The characteristics and activities normally associated with these figures indeed present no obstacle to O'Brien's use of them in his fantastic plots.

> 3. *The use of the fantastic in Menippean satire is internally motivated by the urge to create extraordinary situations for the testing of philosophical ideas. Bakhtin emphasizes that "the fantastic here serves not for the positive embodiment* of truth, but as a mode for searching after truth, provoking it, and most important, testing *it" (114, Bakhtin's emphasis).*

O'Brien's use of the fantastic in some cases seems to be primarily a comic device. However, in other cases, he uses the fantastic precisely in order to set up situations which allow for the interrogation of specific philosophical ideas. For example, the fantastic confrontation between the Pooka McPhellimey and the Good Fairy in *At Swim-Two-Birds* parodies the Cartesian duality of body and mind that is so central to the modern philosophical tradition of the West. Meanwhile, the fantastic afterworld of *The Third Policeman* similarly constitutes a special perspective from which to examine fundamental issues concerning science, religion, and philosophy. The specifically epistemological orientation of this text corresponds well to the interrogation of "truth" indicated by Bakhtin. Similar confrontations with the afterworld also present opportunities for philosophical dialogues in *The Dalkey Archive* as when the appearance of the dead Augustine contributes to important dialogues concerning philosophy and religion, or when the fantastic science of De Selby raises questions regarding the moral responsibility of science. The ostensibly comic motif of the gravid water in *The Hard Life* also raises such questions about science, while at the same time involving the responsibility of the producers and marketers of products concerning the possible results of the uses of those products. Even the "Sea-cat" of *The Poor Mouth* has important philosophical implications. For example, Hunt discusses this creature as a symbol of Ireland and suggests that Bonaparte's failure to confront the Sea-cat shows how the artist who fails to confront and overcome his society's evils becomes part of those evils (Hunt 71).

> 4. *Fantastic and mystical-religious elements are combined with an "extreme crude slum naturalism." "The adventures of truth on earth take place on the high road, in brothels, in the dens of thieves, in taverns, marketplaces, prisons, in erotic orgies of secret cults, and so forth. . . . The organic combination of philosophical dialogue, lofty symbol-systems, the adventure-fantastic, and slum naturalism, is the outstanding characteristic of the menippea" (115).*

O'Brien's work is here again exemplary of the Menippean satire. Together with important philosophical, religious, and mythical material, O'Brien presents in all of his work extensive examples of "crude naturalism." There is no graphic depiction of sexual activity in O'Brien's work, but motifs such as rape and prostitution figure prominently. More importantly, there is a great deal of excremental material in all of his texts. Among other things, O'Brien's texts probably contain more instances of regurgitation than those of any other major writer, recalling the memorable moment in Cervantes's *Don Quixote* when Sancho Panza and Don Quixote inundate one another with vomit. And this parallel is indeed appropriate; O'Brien openly alludes to *Don Quixote* in *The Hard Life* and Bakhtin describes Cervantes's book as one of the "most carnivalistic novels of world literature" (128). But O'Brien's most obvious fellows in this regard are Irish, and he participates in the long Irish tradition of scatological imagery associated with writers like Swift and Joyce.

> 5. *The menippea tends to embody an extreme philosophical universalism and a capacity to contemplate the world on a broad scale and in terms of "ultimate questions" (115).*

Much of the effectiveness of O'Brien's work comes from his focus on specifically Irish issues within Irish settings. But his work frequently addresses issues that are of relevance to a far broader context. His various works interrogate in important ways fundamental and universal issues such as the relationship between truth and fiction or between reality and our linguistic representations of it. *The Third Policeman* is centrally built around the opposition between life and death, perhaps the ultimate of these "ultimate questions." All of O'Brien's texts address questions concerning language and culture that are of the broadest possible relevance.

> 6. *Much of the action of the menippea is transferred from earth to Olympus or to the nether world. Dialogues at the threshold separating different planes of existence—such as the "fabliau of the peasant arguing at the gates of heaven" often appear in the menippea (116).*

Again, O'Brien's participation in this aspect of Menippean satire is obvious. Almost all of *The Third Policeman* takes place in a "nether world," and its reinscription in *The Dalkey Archive* involves visits to a sort of nether world as well. Such texts raise important questions about the threshold between life and the afterlife.

> 7. *The menippea is characterized by a special kind of "experimental fantasticality," which results in a radical change in the scale of the observed phe-*

nomena of life. In particular, the world is often viewed from an unusual perspective, such as from a great height.

O'Brien's work may not involve the obvious changes in scale that occur with the giants of Rabelais or Swift, but his texts do involve a great deal of exaggeration and hyperbole, including at least one giant, the Finn MacCool of *At Swim-Two-Birds*. One thinks here of the extremity of the tortures undergone by Dermot Trellis in *At Swim-Two-Birds* or of the exaggerated squalor of peasant life depicted in *The Poor Mouth*. Other examples of fantastic changes in the normal scale of things in O'Brien's work include the preposterous weight of Mr. Collopy in *The Hard Life* and the powers of the D.M.P. of De Selby in *The Dalkey Archive*. O'Brien often employs unusual and defamiliarizing perspectives on normal life, as in the mixtures of ontological levels in *At Swim* or the view through the afterlife in *The Third Policeman*.

8. *The menippea was the first genre to include a "representation of the unusual, abnormal moral and psychic states of man—insanity of all sorts (the theme of the maniac), split personality, unrestrained daydreaming, unusual dreams, passions bordering on madness, suicides, and so forth" (116).*

One of the most important figures in *At Swim-Two-Birds* is the mad king Sweeney. And near the end of the book, O'Brien presents a disquisition on madness, beginning with the case of Sweeney and asking "Was Hamlet mad? Was Trellis mad? It is extremely hard to say" (314). O'Brien then presents the diagnoses of experts concerning Trellis's mental condition and notes that different people tend to have various sorts of obsessions, ending with the "poor German" obsessed with the number three who commits suicide. Hints of madness run throughout the text of *The Third Policeman* as well, including the explicit case of the ineffable colors produced by Policeman MacCruiskeen, colors that drive anyone who sees them instantly insane. De Selby (in both his incarnations) is a rather mad figure, and the fact that he is also a scientist and philosopher reinforces one of O'Brien's most important points concerning madness— that it is not always that easily distinguishable from rationality. Indeed, O'Brien's depictions of de Selby suggest that excessive reliance on reason and rationality can itself be a form of madness.

9. *Very characteristic are "scandal scenes, eccentric behavior, inappropriate speeches and performances, that is, all sorts of violations of the generally accepted and customary course of events and the established norms of behavior and etiquette, including manners of speech" (117).*

Outrageous and eccentric behavior is quite common for O'Brien's characters. For example, in addition to the elements of madness mentioned above, O'Brien's characters are frequently intoxicated. O'Brien, like Joyce, treats the problem of the excessive consumption of alcohol as a central one in Irish society. O'Brien characters also often engage in criminal acts like the murder of Mathers by the narrator of *The Third Policeman* or the habitual thievery of the Old-Fellow of *The Poor Mouth*. Unusual or exaggerated speech patterns are also prominent in O'Brien's work, which maintains a central focus on language. For example, Werner Huber discusses the way in which O'Brien's use of the grotesque extends to language itself, especially in *The Third Policeman*. Huber also notes how the language of the policemen in this book is "characterized by premeditated stylistic clumsiness, overdetermination and violation of grammatical rules" (123). Thus, for Huber "O'Brien's comic method relies heavily on the technique of stretching language to the breaking-point where convention and misuse meet" (125). O'Brien's work also frequently violates the normal rules and conventions of fiction, as in the confusion between authors and characters in *At Swim-Two-Birds*.

10. *"The menippea is full of sharp contrasts and oxymoronic combinations"* (118).

O'Brien makes important use of such contrasts and striking juxtapositions, such as the opposition between the physical and the spiritual in the confrontation of the Pooka McPhellimey and the Good Fairy in *At Swim-Two-Birds*. Other such oppositions include that between the everyday contemporary world and the world of ancient myth in *At Swim*, between human and animal in *The Poor Mouth*, or between the fantastic and the scholarly in *The Third Policeman*. Surprising oxymoronic combinations are also effectively used by O'Brien, as in the presentation of Joyce as a humble, devout Catholic in *The Dalkey Archive*, or in the depiction of the spiritual Good Fairy in *At Swim* as a cheater at cards.

11. *The menippea often includes "elements of* social *utopia which are incorporated in the form of dreams or journeys to unknown lands"* (118, Bakhtin's emphasis).

The journey to the undiscovered country of the afterworld in *The Third Policeman* (and to some extent in *The Dalkey Archive*) is the clearest example of this aspect of O'Brien's work. That this afterworld differs so little from everyday life in Ireland demonstrates the particularly critical nature of O'Brien's engagement with utopian visions. In this vein, *At*

Swim-Two-Birds engages in an important dialogue with the utopian tradition of Irish myth, while *The Poor Mouth* deconstructs the utopian myth of Irish peasant life. Further, the various schemes of Manus in *The Hard Life* have utopian aspects. In one of his letters to his brother Finbarr, Manus notes that he is hoping to build a better world, "not really a Utopia but a society in which all *unnecessary* wrongs, failures, and misbehaviours are removed" (83, O'Brien's emphasis). But Manus's schemes really amount to venal attempts to increase his own wealth, echoing O'Brien's critical engagement with utopian visions in general.

12. *There is characteristically a wide use of "inserted genres: novellas, letters, oratorical speeches, symposia, and so on; also characteristic is a mixing of prose and poetic speech" (118).*

O'Brien's works quite frequently include such inserted fragments, as in the letters of Manus in *The Hard Life,* the inserted speeches at the Gaelic feist in *The Poor Mouth,* or the numerous footnotes that accompany the main text of *The Third Policeman.* The most obvious examples of this use of inserted genres and fragments occur in *At Swim-Two—Birds,* which is constructed specifically as a patchwork of fragments labeled with italicized headings. Moreover, these fragments are derived from a number of different sources, including letters, newspaper reports, and other books. Sheridan documents that this book was literally constructed as a collage of materials from various sources (45). In addition, the mixture of the poetic world of Irish myth with the prosaic one of everyday life in modern Dublin participates in this motif.

13. *The menippea is typically multi-styled and multi-toned.*

In connection with the patchwork construction of *At Swim-Two-Birds,* Anne Clissmann counts a total of forty-two textual extracts within *At Swim,* combined with a total of thirty-six different styles (86). Similar mixtures of poetic, scientific, philosophical, vulgar, and various other styles occur throughout O'Brien's work.

14. *The menippea is generally concerned with current and topical issues. For example, the satires of Lucian are "full of overt and hidden polemics with various philosophical, religious, ideological and scientific schools, and with the tendencies and currents of his time" (118).*

O'Brien's work frequently engages quite specific topical issues within his contemporary Irish context, including the treatment of women in Irish society, the problem of alcoholism in Ireland, and the Irish "language question." As with Joyce, there is a great deal of dialogue in O'Brien with the power structures of the Catholic Church and the British Empire. There are also dialogues in O'Brien's works with developments in contemporary science, as in *The Third Policeman,* and with specific philosophical systems, as with the case of Augustine and Descartes in *The Dalkey Archive.*

Works Cited

Adorno, Theodor. *Prisms*. Trans. Samuel Weber and Sherry Weber. Cambridge, MA: MIT Press, 1981.

Ahl, Frederick. "Ars Est Caelare Artem (Art in Puns and Anagrams Engraved)." In *On Puns: The Foundation of Letters*. Ed. Jonathan Culler. London: Basil Blackwell, 1988, 17–43.

Asbee, Sue. *Flann O'Brien*. Boston: Twayne, 1991.

Bakhtin, Mikhail. *The Dialogic Imagination*. Ed. Michael Holquist. Trans. Caryl Emerson and Michael Holquist. Austin; U of Texas P, 1981.

———. *Problems of Dostoevsky's Poetics*. Trans. and Ed. Caryl Emerson. Minneapolis: U of Minnesota P, 1984.

———. *Rabelais and His World*. Trans. Helene Iswolsky. Bloomington: Indiana UP, 1984.

———. *Speech Genres and Other Late Essays*. Trans. Vern W. McGhee. Ed. Caryl Emerson and Michael Holquist. Austin: U of Texas P, 1986.

Barolini, Teodolinda. *Dante's Poets: Textuality and Truth in the "Comedy"*. Princeton: Princeton UP, 1984.

Beckett, Samuel. *Disjecta*. New York: Grove, 1984.

———. *First Love and Other Shorts*. New York: Grove, 1974.

———. *Mercier and Camier*. New York: Grove, 1974.

———. *Murphy*. New York: Grove, 1957.

———. *Stories and Texts for Nothing*. New York: Grove, 1967.

———. *Three Novels:* Molloy, Malone Dies, *and* The Unnameable. New York: Grove, 1965.

———. *Waiting for Godot*. New York: Grove, 1954.

———. *Watt*. New York: Grove, 1953.

Beebe, Maurice. *Ivory Towers and Sacred Founts*. New York: New York UP, 1964.

Beitchman, Philip. *I Am a Process with No Subject*. Gainesville: U of Florida P, 1988.

Benstock, Shari. "At the Margin of Discourse: Footnotes in the Fictional Text." *PMLA* 98 (1983): 204–25.

Ben-Zvi, Linda. "Samuel Beckett, Fritz Mauthner, and the Limits of Language." *PMLA* 95 (1980): 183–200.

Bergson, Henri. *Creative Evolution.* Trans. Arthur Mitchell. New York: Modern Library, 1944.

Bernstein, Michael André. "The Poetics of *Ressentiment.*" In *Rethinking Bakhtin: Extensions and Challenges.* Evanston, IL: Northwestern UP, 1989, 197–223.

——. "When the Carnival Turns Bitter: Preliminary Reflections upon the Abject Hero." In *Bakhtin: Essays and Dialogues on His Work.* Chicago: U of Chicago P, 1986, 99–121.

Booker, M. Keith. "The Baby in the Bathwater: Joyce, Gilbert, and Feminist Criticism." *Texas Studies in Literature and Language* 32 (1990): 446–67.

——. "*Finnegans Wake* and *The Satanic Verses:* Two Modern Myths of the Fall." *Critique* 32 (Spring 1991): 190–207.

——. "History and Language in Joyce's 'The Sisters'." *Criticism* 33 (Spring 1991): 217–33.

——. "The Horror of Mortality: Conrad's Dialogue with Master in *Heart of Darkness. Arkansas Quarterly* 2.1 (1993): 1–29.

——. *Literature and Domination: Sex, Knowledge, and Power in Modern Fiction.* Gainsville: UP of Florida, 1993.

——. *Joyce, Bakhtin, and the Literary Tradition.* Ann Arbor: U of Michigan P, forthcoming.

——. "'Nothing That Is So Is So': Dialogic Discourse and the Voice of the Woman in *The Clerk's Tale* and *Twelfth Night. Exemplaria* 3.2 (1991): 519–37.

——. "The Rats of God: Pynchon, Joyce, Beckett, and the Carnivalization of Religion." *Pynchon Notes* 24–25 (1989): 21–30.

Booker, M. Keith. *Techniques of Subversion in Modern Literature: Transgression, Abjection, and the Carnivalesque.* Gainesville: U of Florida P, 1991.

Bohr, Niels. *Atomic Physics and Human Knowledge.* New York: Wiley, 1958.

Borges, Jorge Luis. *Labyrinths.* Ed. Donald A. Yates and James E. Irby. New York: New Directions, 1964.

Breazeale, Daniel, ed. *Philosophy and Truth: Selections from Nietzsche's Notebooks of the Early 1870's.* Trans. Daniel Breazeale. Atlantic Highlands, NJ: Humanities Press, 1979.

Browne, Joseph. "Flann O'Brien: *Post* Joyce or *Propter* Joyce?" *Eire-Ireland* 19 (Winter 1984): 148–57.

Bulgakov, Mikhail. *The Master and Margarita.* Trans. Mirra Ginsberg. New York: Grove Weidenfeld, 1987.

Buttigieg, Joseph A. *"A Portrait of the Artist"* In Different Perspective. Athens: Ohio UP, 1987.

Clark, Katerina, and Michael Holquist. *Mikhail Bakhtin.* Cambridge, MA: Belknap, 1984.

Clissmann, Anne. *Flann O'Brien: A Critical Introduction to His Writings.* New York: Barnes and Noble, 1975.

Cohn, Ruby. "Joyce and Beckett, Irish Cosmopolitans." *James Joyce Quarterly* 8 (1971): 385–91.

————. "*Watt* in the Light of *The Castle*." *Comparative Literature* 13 (1961): 154–66.

Conniff, Brian. "The Dark Side of Magical Realism: Science, Oppression, and Apocalypse in *One Hundred Years of Solitude*. *Modern Fiction Studies* 36 (Summer 1990): 167–79.

Conrad, Joseph. *Heart of Darkness*. In "*Heart of Darkness*" *and* "*The Secret Sharer*". New York: New American Library, 1950.

Cosgrove, Brian. Rev. of *Flann O'Brien: A Critical Introduction to His Writings*, by Anne Clissmann. *Irish University Review* 6.1 (1976): 122–24.

Cunningham, Valentine. "Renoving That Bible: The Absolute Text of (Post) Modernism." In *The Theory of Reading*. Ed. Frank Gloversmith. New York: Barnes and Noble, 1984, 1–51.

Dante Alighieri. *Paradiso*. Trans. Allen Mandelbaum. Berkeley: U of California P, 1984.

————. *De vulgari eloquentia*. Trans. Sally Purcell as *Literature in the Vernacular*. Manchester: Carcanet New Press, 1981.

de Man, Paul. *The Resistance to Theory*. Minneapolis: U of Minnesota P, 1986.

Doherty, Francis. "Flann O'Brien's Existentialist Hell." *Canadian Journal of Irish Studies* 15.2 (1989): 51–67.

Eagleton, Terry. *Walter Benjamin: Towards a Revolutionary Criticism*. London: Verso, 1981.

Edwards, T. R. N. *Three Russian Writers and the Irrational: Zamyatin, Pil'nyak, and Bulgakov*. Cambridge: Cambridge UP, 1982.

Flaubert, Gustave. *Madame Bovary*. Trans. Paul de Man based on the translation by Eleanor Marx Aveling. New York: Norton, 1965.

Fletcher, John. *The Novels of Samuel Beckett*. 2nd ed. New York: Barnes and Noble, 1970.

Foucault, Michel. *The Care of the Self*. Trans. Robert Hurley. New York: Vintage, 1988.

————. *The History of Sexuality, Volume I: An Introduction*. Trans. Robert Hurley. New York: Vintage, 1980.

————. *The Order of Things*. Trans. anonymous. New York: Pantheon Books, 1970.

Fowler, Alastair. "The Future of Genre Theory: Functions and Constructional Types." In *The Future of Literary Theory*. Ed. Ralph Cohen. New York: Routledge, 1989, 291–303.

Frye, Northrop. *Anatomy of Criticism*. Princeton: Princeton UP, 1957.

Fuentes, Carlos. "The Other K." *Tri-Quarterly* 51 (Spring 1981): 256–75.

Gallagher, Monique. "*The Poor Mouth*: Flann O'Brien and the Gaeltacht." *Studies* 72 (Autumn 1983): 231–41.

Gamow, George. *Mr Tompkins in Paperback*. Cambridge: Cambridge UP, 1965.

García Márquez, Gabriel. *One Hundred Years of Solitude*. Trans. Gregory Rabassa. New York: Avon, 1971.

Gifford, Don. *Joyce Annotated: Notes for "Dubliners" and "A Portrait of the Artist as a Young Man"*. Berkeley: U of California P, 1982.

Gluck, Barbara Reich. *Beckett and Joyce: Friendship and Fiction*. Lewisburg, PA: Bucknell UP, 1979.

Granier, Jean. "Nietzsche's Conception of Chaos." *The New Nietzsche: Contemporary Styles of Interpretation*. Ed. David B. Allison. New York: Delta, 1977, 135–41.

Hart, Clive. *Structure and Motif in Finnegans Wake*. Evanston, IL: Northwestern UP, 1962.

Hawthorn, Jeremy. *Joseph Conrad: Language and Fictional Self-Consciousness*. Lincoln: U of Nebraska P, 1979.

Hayman, David. "Joyce—Beckett/Joyce." In *The Seventh of Joyce*. Ed. Bernard Benstock. Bloomington: Indiana UP, 1982, 37–43.

Hayman, David "A Meeting in the Park and a Meeting on the Bridge: Joyce and Beckett." *James Joyce Quarterly* (1971): 372–84.

———. *Re-Forming the Narrative: Toward a Mechanics of Modernist Fiction*. Ithaca: Cornell UP, 1987.

Heidegger, Martin. "The Origin of the Work of Art," in *Basic Writings from "Being and Time" (1927) to "The Task of Thinking" (1964)*. Ed. David Farrell Krell. New York: Harper and Row, 1977, 3–35.

Heisenberg, Werner. *Across the Frontiers*. New York: Harper and Row, 1974.

———. *Physics and Philosophy*. New York: Harper and Row, 1958.

Henke, Suzette. "Stephen Dedalus and Women: A Portrait of the Artist as a Young Misogynist." In *Women in Joyce*. Ed. Suzette Henke and Elaine Unkeless. Urbana: U of Illinois P, 1982, 82–107.

Henning, Sylvie Debevec. *Beckett's Critical Complicity: Carnival, Contestation, and Tradition*. Lexington: UP of Kentucky, 1988.

Henry, P. L. "The Structure of Flann O'Brien's *At Swim-Two-Birds*." *Irish University Review* 20.1 (1990): 35–40.

Herr, Cheryl. *Joyce's Anatomy of Culture*. Urbana: U of Illinois P, 1986.

Hirschkop, Ken, ed. *Bakhtin and Cultural Theory*. Manchester: Manchester UP, 1989.

Holquist, Michael. *Dialogism: Bakhtin and His World*. London: Routledge, 1990.

Hooker, Clifford A. "The Nature of Quantum Mechanical Reality: Einstein Versus Bohr." In *Paradigms and Paradoxes: The Philosophical Challenge of the Quantum Domain*. Ed. Robert G. Colodny. Pittsburgh: U of Pittsburgh P, 1972, 67–209.

Horkheimer, Max, and Theodor W. Adorno. *Dialectic of Enlightenment*. Trans. John Cumming. New York: Seabury, 1972.

Huber, Werner. "Flann O'Brien and the Language of the Grotesque." In *Anglo-Irish and Irish Literature: Aspects of Language and Culture*. Ed. Birgit Bramsbäck and Martin Croghan. Uppsala: Uppsala UP, 1988, 123–30.

Hunt, Roy L. "Hell Goes Round and Round: Flann O'Brien." *Canadian Journal of Irish Studies* 14.2 (1989): 60–73.

Huxley, Aldous. *Point Counter Point*. New York: Harper and Row, 1965.

Imhof, Rüdiger. "Two Meta-Novelists: Sternesque Elements in Novels by Flann O'Brien." In *"Alive-Alive O!": Flann O'Brien's "At Swim-Two-Birds"*. Ed. Rüdiger Imhof. Dublin: Wolfhound, 1985, 160–90.

Janik, Del Ivan. "Flann O'Brien: The Novelist as Critic." *Eire-Ireland* 4 (1969): 64–72.

Joyce, James. *The Collected Letters of James Joyce*. Vol. I. Ed. Stuart Gilbert. London: Faber, 1957.

———. *"Dubliners": Text, Criticism, and Notes*. Ed. Robert Scholes and A. Walton Litz. New York: Viking, 1969.

———. *Finnegans Wake*. New York: Viking, 1939.

———. *"A Portrait of the Artist as a Young Man": Text, Criticism, and Notes*. Ed. Chester G. Anderson. New York: Viking, 1968.

———. *Stephen Hero*. Edited from Manuscripts by Theodore Spencer. Additional Manuscript Pages Edited by John J. Slocum and Herbert Cahoon. New York: New Directions, 1963.

———. *"Ulysses": The Corrected Text*. Ed. Hans Walter Gabler with Wolfhard Steppe and Claus Melchior. New York: Random House, 1986.

Juraga, Dubravka, and M. Keith Booker. "Literature, Power, and Oppression in Stalinist Russia and Catholic Ireland: Danilo Kis's Use of Joyce in *A Tomb for Boris Davidovich*. Unpublished essay, U of Arkansas.

Kafka, Franz. *The Castle*. Trans. Willa Muir and Edwin Muir. New York: Schocken, 1954.

Kemnitz, Charles. "Beyond the Zone of the Middle Dimensions: A Relativistic Reading of *The Third Policeman*." *Irish University Review* 15.1 (1985): 56–72.

Kenner, Hugh. "The Cubist *Portrait*." In *Approaches to Joyce's* Portrait." Ed. Thomas F. Staley and Bernard Benstock. Pittsburgh: U of Pittsburgh P, 1976, 171–84.

———. *Dublin's Joyce*. New York: Columbia UP, 1987.

———. *Samuel Beckett: A Critical Study*. 2nd ed. Berkeley: U of California P, 1968.

———. *The Stoic Comedians: Flaubert, Joyce, and Beckett*. Berkeley: U of California P, 1974.

Kershner, R. B., Jr. "A French Connection: Iris Murdoch and Raymond Queneau." *Éire-Ireland* 18 (Winter 1983–84): 144–56.

———. "Joyce and Queneau as Novelists." Diss. Stanford U, 1972.

———. *Joyce, Bakhtin, and Popular Literature: Chronicles of Disorder*. Chapel Hill: U of North Carolina P, 1989.

Klinkowitz, Jerome. "*At Swim-Two-Birds* by Flann O'Brien." *The New Republic* (August 16 and 23): 31–33.

Knowlson, James, ed. *Samuel Beckett: An Exhibition*. London: Turret Books, 1971.

Kristeva, Julia. *Powers of Horror*. Trans. Leon S. Roudiez. New York: Columbia UP, 1982.

———. "Word, Dialogue, and Novel." In *Desire in Language: A Semiotic Approach to Literature and Art*. Trans. Thomas Gora, Alice Jardine, and Leon S, Roudiez. Ed. Leon S. Roudiez. New York: Columbia UP, 1980, 64–91.

Lacan, Jacques. *Écrits: A Selection*. Trans. Alan Sheridan. New York: Norton, 1977.

Langbaum, Robert. "The Mysteries of Identity: A Theme in Modern Literature." In his *The Modern Spirit*. New York: Oxford UP, 1970, 164–84.

Lanters, José. "Fiction Within Fiction: The Role of the Author in Flann O'Brien's *At Swim-Two-Birds* and *The Third Policeman*." *Dutch Quarterly Review of Anglo-American Letters* 13.4 (1983): 267–81.

Levitt, Morton P. "From Realism to Magic Realism: The Meticulous Modernist Fictions of García Márquez." In *Critical Perspectives on Gabriel García Márquez*. Ed. Bradley A. Shaw and Nora Vera-Godwin. Lincoln, NE, Society of Spanish and Spanish-American Studies, 1986, 73–89.

Lodge, David. "Double Discourses: Joyce and Bakhtin." *James Joyce Broadsheet* 11 (1983): 1.

Mackenzie, Ian. "Who's Afraid of James Joyce? Or, Flann O'Brien's Retreat from Modernism." *Etudes de Lettres*. No. 1 (1983): 55–67.

McGuire, Jerry L. "Teasing after Death: Metatextuality in *The Third Policeman*." *Éire-Ireland* 16.2 (1981): 107–21.

McNab, Gregory. "The Hard Life: Gaelic Autobiography and the Image of the Irish Language." *Éire-Ireland* 14.3 (1979): 133–41.

Mailloux, Steven. *Interpretive Conventions: The Reader in the Study of American Fiction*. Ithaca: Cornell UP, 1982.

Manganiello, Dominic. *Joyce's Politics*. London: Routledge, 1980.

Marzorati, Gerald. "Salman Rushdie: Fiction's Embattled Infidel." *New York Times Magazine* (Jan. 29, 1989): 25 + .

Mays, J. C. C. "Brian O'Nolan and Joyce on Art and on Life." *James Joyce Quarterly* 11 (1974): 238–56.

Mellamphy, Ninian. "Aestho-Autogamy and the Anarchy of Imagination: Flann O'Brien's Theory of Fiction in *At Swim-Two-Birds*." In *"Alive-Alive O!": Flann O'Brien's "At Swim-Two-Birds"*. Ed. Rüdiger Imhof. Dublin: Wolfhound, 1985, 140–60.

Mendilow, A. A. *Time and the Novel*. New York: Humanities, 1972.

Mercier, Vivian. *Beckett/Beckett*. New York: Oxford UP, 1977.

———. *The Irish Comic Tradition*. Oxford: Clarendon, 1962.

Miller, J. Hillis. *Fiction and Repetition: Seven English Novels*. Cambridge, MA: Harvard UP, 1982.

Moorjani, Angela B. *Abysmal Games in the Novels of Samuel Beckett*. Chapel Hill: U of North Carolina P, 1982.

Morson, Gary Saul, ed. *Bakhtin: Essays and Dialogues on His Work*. Chicago: U of Chicago P, 1986.

———and Caryl Emerson. *Mikhail Bakhtin: Creation of a Prosaics*. Stanford, CA: Stanford UP, 1990.

———and Caryl Emerson, eds. *Rethinking Bakhtin: Extensions and Challenges*. Evanston, Illinois: Northwestern University Press, 1989.

Moses, Michael Valdez. "The Sadly Rejoycing Slave: Beckett, Joyce, and Destructive Parody." *Modern Fiction Studies* 31 (1985): 659–74.

Nänny, Max. "*The Waste Land*: A Menippean Satire?" *English Studies* 66 (1985): 526–35.

Nietzsche, Friedrich. *Beyond Good and Evil: Basic Writings of Nietzsche*. Trans. and ed. Walter Kaufmann. New York: Modern Library, 1968, 181–435.

————. *The Gay Science.* Trans. Walter Kaufmann. New York: Vintage Books–Random House, 1974.

————. "On Truth and Lies in a Nonmoral Sense." In *Philosophy and Truth: Selections from Nietzsche's Notebooks of the Early 1870's.* Trans. and ed. Daniel Breazeale. Atlantic Highlands, NJ: Humanities, 1979, 79–97.

————. *The Will to Power.* Trans. Walter Kaufmann and R. J. Hollingdale. Ed. Walter Kaufmann. New York: Vintage Books–Random House, 1968.

O'Brien, Flann. "A Bash in the Tunnel." In *Stories and Plays.* New York: Viking, 1973, 201–8.

————. *At Swim-Two-Birds.* New York: New American Library, 1976.

————. (as Myles na Gopaleen). *The Best of Myles.* Ed. Kevin O'Nolan. New York: Penguin, 1983.

————. *The Dalkey Archive.* New York: Macmillan, 1965.

————. *The Hard Life: An Exegesis of Squalor.* London: Picador, 1976.

————. *The Poor Mouth: A Bad Story about the Hard Life.* Trans. Patrick Power. New York: Seaver, 1981.

————. *The Third Policeman.* New York: New American Library, 1967.

O'Toole, Mary. "The Theory of Serialism in *The Third Policeman.*" *Irish University Review* 18 (1988): 215–25.

Palmeri, Frank. *Satire in Narrative: Petronius, Swift, Gibbon, Melville, and Pynchon.* Austin: U of Texas P, 1990.

Peppard, Victor. *The Poetics of Yury Olesha.* Gainesville: U of Florida P, 1989.

Politzer, Heinz. "The Wall of Secrecy: Kafka's *Castle.*" In *Franz Kafka: Modern Critical Views.* Ed. Harold Bloom. New York: Chelsea House, 1986, 33–52.

Power, Arthur. *Conversations with James Joyce.* Ed. Clive Hart. Chicago: U of Chicago P, 1974.

Power, Mary. "Flann O'Brien and Classical Satire: An Exegesis of *The Hard Life.*" *Éire-Ireland* 13.1 (1978): 87–102.

Queneau, Raymond. *The Flight of Icarus.* Trans. Barbara Wright. New York: New Directions, 1973.

Ricoeur, Paul. *Time and Narrative.* Vol. III. Trans. Kathleen Blamey and David Pellauer. Chicago: U of Chicago P, 1988.

Rorty, Richard. *Consequences of Pragmatism.* Minneapolis: U of Minnesota P, 1982.

————. *Philosophy and the Mirror of Nature.* Princeton, Princeton UP, 1979.

Rushdie, Salman. "The Empire Writes Back with a Vengeance." *London Times* (July 3, 1982): 8.

————. "In Good Faith." *Newsweek* (Feb. 12, 1990): 52–57.

————. *The Satanic Verses.* New York: Viking, 1989.

Schwartz, Sanford. *The Matrix of Modernism: Pound, Eliot, and Twentieth Century Thought.* Princeton: Princeton UP, 1985.

Shea, Thomas F. "The Craft of Seeming Pedestrian: Flann O'Brien's *The Hard Life.*" *Colby Library Quarterly* 25.4 (1989): 258–67.

Sheridan, Niall. "Brian, Flann and Myles." In *Myles: Portraits of Brian O'Nolan.* Ed. Timothy O'Keefe. London: Martin Brian and O'Keefe, 1973, 32–53.

Shoaf, R. A. "The Play of Puns in Late Middle English Poetry: Concerning

Juxtology." In *On Puns: The Foundation of Letters.* Ed. Jonathan Culler. London: Basil Blackwell, 1988, 44–61.

Silverthorne, J. M. "Time, Literature, and Failure: Flann O'Brien's *At Swim-Two-Birds* and *The Third Policeman. Éire-Ireland* 11.4 (1976): 66–83.

Smith, Johanna M. "'Too Beautiful Altogether': Patriarchal Ideology in *Heart of Darkness.*" In *"Heart of Darkness": A Case Study in Contemporary Criticism.* Ed. Ross C. Murfin. New York: St. Martin's, 1989, 179–95.

Sorrentino, Gilbert. *Mulligan Stew.* New York: Grove, 1979.

Spears, Monroe K. *Dionysus and the City: Modernism in Twentieth-Century Poetry.* New York: Oxford UP, 1970.

Stallybrass, Peter, and Allon White. *The Politics and Poetics of Transgression.* Ithaca: Cornell UP, 1986.

Stevens, Wallace. *The Collected Poems.* New York: Knopf, 1954.

——. *The Necessary Angel: Essays on Reality and the Imagination.* New York: Knopf, 1951.

Stevick, Philip. "Novel and Anatomy: Notes Toward an Amplification of Frye." *Criticism* 10 (1968): 153–65.

Thiher, Allen. *Words in Reflection: Modern Language Theory and Postmodern Fiction.* Chicago: U of Chicago P, 1984.

Titunik, I. R. "Mikhail Zoshchenko and the Problem of *Skaz.*" *California Slavic Studies* 6 (1971): 83–96.

Todorov, Tzvetan. *Mikhail Bakhtin and the Dialogical Principle.* Trans. Wlad Godzich. Minneapolis: U of Minnesota P, 1984.

Ulmer, Gregory L. "The Object of Post-Criticism" In *The Anti-Aesthetic: Essays on Postmodern Culture.* Ed. Hal Foster. Port Townsend, WA: Bay, 1983, 83–110.

Ungar, Andras. "Among the Hapsburgs: Arthur Griffith, Stephen Dedalus, and the Myth of Bloom." *Twentieth Century Literature* 35 (1989): 480–501.

Valente, Joseph. "The Politics of Joyce's Polyphony." In *New Alliances in Joyce Studies: "When It's Aped to Foul a Delfian".* Ed. Bonnie Kime Scott. Newark, DE: U of Delaware P, 1988, 56–68.

Voelker, Joseph C. "'Doublends Jined': The Fiction of Flann O'Brien." *Journal of Irish Literature* 12.1 (1983): 87–95.

White, Allon. "Bakhtin, Sociolinguistics and Deconstruction." In *The Theory of Reading.* Ed. Frank Gloversmith. New York: Barnes and Noble, 1984, 123–46.

——. "Pigs and Pierrots: The Politics of Transgression in Modern Fiction." *Raritan* 11 (1982): 51–70.

Wright, A. Colin. *Mikhail Bulgakov: Life and Interpretations.* Toronto: U of Toronto P, 1978.

Wright, Barbara. Translator's note. *The Flight of Icarus.* By Raymond Queneau. New York: New Directions, 1973, 5–9.

Yaeger, Patricia. *Honey-Mad Women: Emancipatory Strategies in Women's Writing.* New York: Columbia UP, 1988.

Index

Abject imagery, 10, 71, 77, 107
Adorno, Theodor, 95, 130–32
Ahl, Frederick, 32
Alienation, 18, 22, 68, 73, 127, 137
Allegory, 28, 127, 138
Asbee, Sue, 69, 122
Augustine, Saint, 20, 108–11, 116, 145, 150
Authorial intention, 33, 40, 44, 45

Bakhtin, Mikhail, 1–7, 11, 31, 44, 67, 71, 76, 82, 105, 135; *The Dialogic Imagination*, 3, 31, 69, 70, 120, 144; *Problems of Dostoevsky's Poetics*, 1, 46, 137, 143–50; *Rabelais and His World*, 4, 47, 60; *Speech Genres and Other Late Essays*, 32, 83. *See also* Carnivalesque imagery; Catholicism; Dialogism; History; Menippean satire; Parody; Polyphony
Bakunin, Mikhail, 135
Barolini, Teodolinda, 45
Beckett, Samuel, 1, 4, 7–27, 47, 49, 66–68, 84, 102, 105, 106, 111, 121, 124, 125, 129–33; "The End," 79; *Endgame*, 106; "First Love," 26; *Malone Dies*, 8, 10, 16, 17, 19, 25, 80; *Mercier and Camier*, 10, 21, 22, 24; *Molloy*, 11, 14–16, 19, 20, 22, 24, 25, 68; *Murphy*, 8, 9, 11, 21, 27; *Texts for Nothing*, 18; *The Unnamable*,

14, 16, 17, 21, 68; *Waiting for Godot*, 77; *Watt*, 9, 10, 14, 22, 27, 49, 68, 84, 125, 129, 131, 132
Beebe, Maurice, 16
Beitchman, Philip, 26
Benstock, Shari, 49
Ben-Zvi, Linda, 22
Bergson, Henri, 51, 52, 107
Bernstein, Michael André, 4
Bohr, Niels, 55, 56
Booker, M. Keith, 4, 12, 13, 31, 77, 88, 100, 115, 123, 132, 133, 135
Borges, Jorge Luis, 58, 79, 121
Breazeale, Daniel, 62
Bricolage, 30, 32, 101, 114, 123. *See also* Collage
Browne, Joseph, 11, 16, 50
Browning, Robert, 87
Bulgakov, Mikhail, 7, 136–39
Buttigieg, Joseph, 107

Čapek, Karel, 126
Carnivalesque imagery, 1–6, 20, 44, 47, 60, 71, 78, 82, 101–3, 143, 144
Cartesian thought, 17–21, 23–26, 47, 48, 110, 145. *See also* Descartes, René
Catholicism, 28, 39, 135; Bakhtin on, 60; Joyce and, 14, 40, 69, 74, 92, 93, 98, 105, 114; and language, 36, 45; O'Brien's, 9, 40, 105; O'Brien's criticism of, 40, 86, 91–93, 102,

159

Irish
Studies

Richard Fallis, *Series Editor*

Irish Studies presents a wide range of books interpreting important aspects of Irish life and culture to scholarly and general audiences. The richness and complexity of the Irish experience, past and present, deserve broad understanding and careful analysis. For this reason, an important purpose of the series is to offer a forum to scholars interested in Ireland, its history, and culture. Irish literature is a special concern in the series, but works from the perspectives of the fine arts, history, and the social sciences are also welcome, as are studies that take multidisciplinary approaches.

Selected titles in the series include:

www.ingramcontent.com/pod-product-compliance
Lightning Source LLC
Chambersburg PA
CBHW030307100426
42812CB00002B/605